Tea Time

Tea Time
The Art of Taking Tea

Text Marie Simon
Photography Marie-Pierre Morel
Illustrations Hélène Le Duff
Food styling Christèle Ageorges

NEW YORK · LONDON

The Taste of Tea

...

Tea is back in fashion, but for a time-honored establishment like Ladurée, fashion is irrelevant. For Ladurée, tea defies trends. It is a fragile, delicate entity, providing a moment beyond time; it is the fruit of emotion, talent and perseverance, the lifeblood of friendship, and an inexhaustible source of creativity and passion.
A cup of tea contains the flavors of the world.

Ladurée's tearooms have always strived to extol the wonders of tea and its French-style service, and in these pages we set out to share the world of Ladurée tea, our historic tearooms and their delicious creations. It is a labor of love, a eulogy to the leaf and the gourmet magic of pastry and gateaux. Each of our teas is the perfect accompaniment for a sweet or savory creation. Our teas are an expression of their historical tradition. Each has been carefully blended to achieve subtle aromas, sensual flavors, daringly pairing the unorthodox with the sublime. Each tea is a journey to faraway lands; often they are tributes to historical figures or charismatic characters of fiction; each tea contains within it the memory of something precious and unforgettable.

Whether served in a mug or porcelain cup, with or without milk, chilled or piping hot, delicately light or full-bodied, tea is a ritual, a moment to be shared among friends. It is a mysterious, fragile libation that requires a therapeutic degree of care and attention. It has many virtues, one of the most vital of which is its appeal to the imagination.

Tea provides an enchanting moment of calm and tranquility, a vision of paradise. It is the key to creating a different life based on fascinating flavors and inner-peace.

Contents

...

History in a Tea Cup
PAGE 8

IMPERIAL TEA
PAGE 14

BRITISH TEA
PAGE 40

TEA AND BRUNCH
PAGE 76

ROYAL TEA
PAGE 102

TEA IN THE GARDEN
PAGE 144

RUSSIAN TEA
PAGE 174

TEA AND TRAVEL
PAGE 202

TEA IN LOVE
PAGE 232

TEA PARTY
PAGE 266

Basic Recipes
PAGE 296

The Ladurée Tea Collection
PAGE 303

Index
PAGE 306

Acknowledgments
PAGE 307

History in a Tea Cup

"There is a subtle charm in the taste of tea which makes it irresistible and capable of idealization. [...] It has not the arrogance of wine, the self-consciousness of coffee, nor the simpering innocence of cocoa."
Okakura Kakuzō, The Book of Tea.

THE BENEFITS OF SLEEP

According to Chinese religion, in 2737 BC, the mythical sage ruler Shen Nung woke up and drank a cup of boiling water as was his wont. In his wisdom, he had decreed that all his subjects should boil water before drinking it. This particular morning however leaves of the *Camellia sinensis* tree had fallen into the cauldron as he slept.
As he applied his own wise hygiene policy he also discovered a delectable, restorative tonic. Ever since, the Chinese have revered Shen Nung as the father of tea, agriculture and medicine. His discovery went on to prosper until its widespread adoption as the national beverage during the Tang Dynasty (618–907 AD).
In *The Book of Tea*, Okakura Kakuzō describes each period of tea's development. The Tang dynasty saw the "classic school of tea", a period during which the first tea houses appeared (before 790 AD) and the tea trade flourished, reaching Tibet, Mongolia, Turkey and the Tartars. During this period, tea was prepared by first compressing tea leaves into cakes, which were then boiled.
In his tea bible, *The Classic of Tea*, the Buddhist Monk, Lu Yu (733–804 AD) explains the various types of tea

and their preparation. For Lu Yu however tea meant more: it symbolized the harmony and mysterious unity of the universe.

TEA SCHOOLS

In China, the Song dynasty (960–1279) introduced a new approach to tea drinking, the "romantic school". Tea was ground into a powder and whipped into hot water with a bamboo whisk, then drunk in solid, dark blue or dark brown ceramic bowls. This method moved to Japan, where, as it had under the Tang dynasty, Japan still emulated Chinese civilization and tea was also grown and worshipped by monks. Later under Manchurian domination, the Ming dynasty (1368–1644) introduced what was the third "school of tea", the "naturalistic school". Tea leaves were now steeped in a teapot then drunk in delicate porcelain cups to reveal the beverage's beautiful amber hue. In Japan, Buddhists of the Zen school began to formalize the tea ritual and the 15th century saw the birth of the tea ceremony where powdered Matcha tea was whipped into hot water with a bamboo whisk. The refined minimalism and architectural purity of the tea chamber, created a sanctuary or "Abode of Vacancy", conducive to inner peace. As well as a religion in Japan, tea became an art of living.

THE GOLDEN BEVERAGE

Tea reached the West much later, arriving in the early 17th century. With its reputed therapeutic virtues, which were mainly the stuff of fancy, tea began to win over European elites. The marquise de Sévigné relates how he witnessed an ailing man restored to health after forty cups of tea. Two centuries later, in his novel *Lost Illusions*, Balzac describes how in the provinces, tea was still "sold in apothecaries as indigestion medication."

However, in the 18th century, its medical virtues were overlooked by the French aristocracy who preferred the exotic cachet of what was a luxury product. Such was its prestige that the most illustrious artisans of Europe vied with each other to produce the finest silverware and porcelain to match its eminence.

A STORM IN A TEAPOT

The Portuguese imported tea into Europe. After Vasco de Gama opened the way to India in 1498, bold seafarers ventured further to China and Japan bringing back tea to the court of Portugal. When she married Charles II in 1662, the Portuguese princess Catherine de Bragance introduced it to the court of England. The West first discovered black tea, the leaves of which were steeped in hot water. Green tea and powdered tea were discovered later. The Portuguese monopoly of their discovery did not last long and a bitter war to dominate the tea trade broke out. The Dutch took the lead but were soon outmaneuvered by the English. In the meantime, Japan had closed its borders in 1638, which meant that China was the sole exporter of the precious leaf.

ENGLAND FALLS IN LOVE

The first cargos of tea and porcelain from China were conveyed by Dutch traders first to Amsterdam, then Paris and finally London. The English fell so in love with the new beverage that the nation set about devising fearsome strategies to dominate supply and cash in. They ousted the French and Dutch East India Companies to dominate trade and imposed huge taxes, notably on their colonial cousins in America. Their tea tyranny bore consequences: the Boston Tea Party spawned the American Revolution and the Declaration of Independence in the US, while the Chinese started

growing opium to reduce their trade deficit with the Crown, which led to the two Opium Wars, 1839–1842 and 1856–1860. For the English, tea was absolutely worth all the tea in China, and their love knew no bounds.

THE TEA SPY

Britain's infatuation with their national brew allowed a number of intrepid entrepreneurs to flourish. In 1657, Thomas Garraway inaugurated one of the first tea emporiums in London while in 1706 Thomas Twining opened Tom's Coffee House, before creating a women-only tearoom the following year, a place where women could sally forth alone or with friends without sullying their reputation – coffee houses were the preserve of men. By 1750, English workers and laborers alike were subjugated by its charms and the government was eager to profit from their addiction. The aptly named botanist Robert Fortune pulled off a daring coup of industrial espionage. In 1848, Fortune was sent undercover into China by the British East India Company to discover the secret of tea. The British Empire was eager to put an end to their dependency on a single market in order to grow their own production in India. Between the two Opium Wars, disguised as a local, Fortune infiltrated plantations across China, taking cuttings from tea plants. In his book recounting his success, *Two visits to the tea countries of China and the British tea plantations in the Himalaya; with a narrative of adventures, and a full description of the culture of the tea plant, the agriculture, horticulture, and botany of China* (1853), Fortune tells how he dispatched 20,000 plants and teams of Chinese laborers to plantations in the heart of the Himalayas where his enterprise flourished. Darjeeling tea was born. The English colony of Ceylon soon became England's second colonial tea haven and in the late 19th century, Thomas Lipton bought up the island's former coffee plantations that had been decimated by illness. For this latest venture, he implemented an industrial strategy he had learned from the United States: with the slogan. "From the tea garden to the teapot!" he deployed Lipton-brand packaging to sell his product. The rest, as they say, is history.

THE GOLDEN AGE OF TEAROOMS

Tea again prospered during the Industrial Revolution. In the 19th century, the West began to drink tea on a daily basis as a civilized and sociable pastime. "Afternoon tea" became part of the daily timetable for sustenance and its formalities created new codes of etiquette among polite society on the continent in France, Germany, and Russia. In the second half of the 19th century, tea rooms spread to European capitals. Ernest Ladurée was among the pioneers. His bakery in rue Royale gradually turned into a popular tearoom. Metropolitan tearooms, the city hotspots of their time, were bedecked in luxuriant decor and bespoke furnishings. For their upwardly mobile female clientele in France, the tearoom was a stage on which to display one's wealth and elegance on a par with the Bois de Boulogne, the opera and the theater.
Far from the Japanese tea ceremony and Abodes of Vacancy, in the West, tea finds a different paradoxical expression where a single tea cup contains both cosmic harmony and western resplendence.

Imperial TEA

Imperial Tea

Asia does not drink tea like the rest of the world.
In the Far East, it is common practice to infuse tea-leaves several times.
Tea accessories and tea rituals are different.
The act of tasting tea has spiritual value that does not exist elsewhere.

THE DRINK THAT NEVER STOPS

The Chinese drink tea everywhere, at any moment of the day, and not just jasmine tea. In government meetings, instead of the customary glass of water we might put before officials, you'll find a teacup. The Chinese use bowls, or *zhong*, into which they pour hot water directly onto green tea leaves. The bowls have special lids that filter the leaves when drinking. Throughout the day, the leaves are infused several times. In Japan, even individual leaves may get the hot-water treatment several times.

To fully bring out its sweet, bitter, astringent qualities, Sencha, for example, is generally infused thrice, reducing the brew time with each infusion. As in China, green tea is drunk throughout the day and there are green tea distributors at every street corner.

IN HARMONY WITH NATURE

In the Far East, tea exudes its own subtle fascinating artistry, rooted in its millenarian tradition, and grounded in Taoist and Buddhist teachings. In China and Japan, tea plantations and temples sit side-by-side on the map, because tea rituals were first developed by monks. For the Taoist school, tea symbolizes harmony. During the Tang dynasty, the Chinese monk Lu Yu (733-804) wrote *The Classic of Tea*, a bible of tea culture and philosophy. His poem contemplates tea's relationship with the world. Its plants germinate in the earth and reach for the heavens.

The best water to make tea comes from streams running through plantations. Drinking tea requires a state of inner peace to fully meditate upon its subtle flavors.

TEA AND TEASE

Tea is not a drink like others. Whether in tearooms or at home, drinking tea is a moment of sharing, a ritual to honor a passing guest.
In the 17th century, teahouses were rife in China. To Marco Polo they were dens of iniquity due to the women of easy virtue who frequented them. Centuries later, during the Cultural Revolution, they were deemed frivolous, "non-productive pastimes" and, after one thousand years of continuous service, they were unceremoniously shut down. Today, however, teahouses are back with a vengeance and still respect the tradition of *Gong Fu Cha*.
Unlike Japan's *Chanoyu*, which is a ceremony, Gong Fu Cha is China's precision art of brewing tea.

Rather than let the flavor flood out, the aim is to gently tease out the subtle aromas so that tea can be savored like wine. The preparation involves several short brewing stages lasting 1–2 minutes. The teapot is filled to the brim to let the surface froth overflow. Another important feature of this art is to inhale the aromas of a cup that has just been emptied into another – the theory is that a steaming empty cup provides the best expression of the leaf's delicate fragrances. Each stage is prolonged by ten seconds, conveying different notes. If the tea is of high quality, it can be infused up to fifteen times!

IN THE LAND OF THE RISING SUN

In Japan, tea is an art of living. This refined, sober ritual firmly rooted in Zen Buddhism has influenced many aspects of Japanese culture: architecture, landscape design, incense, the floral art of *ikebana*, ceramics and calligraphy. The tea ceremony was introduced in the 16th century by the great Japanese tea master, Sen no Rikyū, who developed the *cha-no-yu* ritual, based on four principles: *wa* ("harmony"), *kei* ("respect"), *sei* ("purity") and *jaku* ("serenity"). He is also attributed with inventing the Raku ceramic *chawan* bowl and the ceremonial tea room or "Abode of Vacancy", the chamber where the ceremony takes place. His philosophy and ethics are at the origin of the three major Japanese schools of the tea ceremony, which today continue his precepts. The ceremony may appear simple and humble but it has very precise codes.

Here Matcha reigns supreme. It is unique: no other tea in the world comes in powdered form and no other is whipped into the water with a bamboo whisk to obtain that special raw green, liquid jade emulsion, which has the color of tea plantations.
The Japanese expression *Ichigo ichie* – meaning "one time, one meeting" – evokes the concept of treasuring time with people and perfectly describes the tea tasting moment. Each encounter with tea is unique, a moment of intensity and sincerity.

Red Tuna Satay with Sprouted Leeks

Serves 6 people
Preparation: 30 minutes
Marinade: 8–10 hours

14 oz | 400 g red Mediterranean tuna
3 oz | 90 g sprouted leeks
⅓ cup | 50 g crushed peanuts
Fleur de sel (or other coarse sea salt)

Marinade
1 ¼ cup | 30 cl olive oil
½ tbsl | 5 g red satay paste

Satay sauce
¾ cup | 200 ml olive oil
¾ tbsp | 10 g yellow curry paste
2 cups | 500 ml of unsweetened coconut milk
3 tbsp | 50 ml white vinegar
½ tbsp | 5 g brown sugar
2 pinches of table salt

1. Start by preparing the marinade: briskly whisk the olive oil and the red satay paste until smooth. If possible, allow to rest for 6-8 hours before filtering through a fine mesh sieve. The resulting oil will be smooth and red. Pour the marinade into a dish deep enough to hold the fish.

2. Take the tuna loin and cut rectangles weighing approximately 60 g each. Place the cuts in the marinade and allow to rest in the refrigerator covered with plastic wrap for approximately 2 hours.

3. Meanwhile, prepare the satay sauce: heat the olive oil and add the yellow curry paste. Mix well. Add sugar and deglaze the pan with vinegar. Bring to a boil and pour in the coconut milk. Leave to simmer. When oil begins to pool at the surface, remove from heat and whisk the sauce. Season to taste and pour into a clean bowl.

Pairs well with
Our *Lapsang Souchong* tea

4. Remove the tuna from the refrigerator and pour off excess marinade. Sear the fish on a plancha; approximately 2 minutes each side. Ideally, the tuna should still be rare in the middle

5. Heat the satay sauce. Pour a small amount of sauce on a plate. Slice the tuna on the diagonal and carefully arrange over the sauce. Garnish with leek sprouts and finish with a sprinkle of chopped peanuts and a pinch of *fleur de sel*.

Chef's tip

When buying tuna, choose one that has been fished responsibly. The fish should carry a ring indicating where it was caught. You can also opt for either the MSC or ASC labels. They ensure that the product has been sustainably fished or farmed.

TEA ALCHEMY

The key to tea's flavor and color is oxidation, or fermentation – and it is essential to production.

ALL IN THE ENZYME

Oxidation is a natural process: as plants mature they wither in contact with the air and their pigmentation changes. When leaves are naturally or artificially withered, their cell walls break down and oxidase is released, the enzyme responsible for oxidation and fermentation. Oxidase then transforms the catechins of polyphenols (or tannins) into two molecules that produce fermented teas' distinctive brown color.

CONTROLLED AGING

Black teas undergo complete oxidation in five stages: the leaves are allowed to wither and dehydrate; they are rolled to break down the cells; oxidation then takes place in chambers with humidity levels of 90 or 95%; they are then dried in ovens to halt oxidation, before being sorted and sifted. Green teas undergo a different process. Leaves are dried using short bursts of intense heat which kills the enzymes responsible for oxidation. After the leaves have been rolled they are dried once more then sorted into grades. Oolong teas are semi-fermented. Their fermentation is halted with intense heat that also prevents the reaction of enzymes, similar to the process for green teas.

Scallop Carpaccio

Serves 6 people
Preparation: 40 minutes
Refrigeration: several hours

18 scallops
1 large Meyer lemon
1 lime (juice and zest of)
1 green apple
3 slices of bread
½ cup | 100 ml organic oil
1 pinch of ground Espelette pepper (or hot Paprika)
3 pinches of *fleur de sel* (or other coarse sea salt)

Pickled radishes
1 bunch of round, red radishes (approximately 12)
2 cups | 500 ml white vinegar
2 cups | 500 ml red wine vinegar
4 tbsp | 50 g granulated sugar

1. Start by preparing the pickles. Wash and cut the radishes into 8–12 pieces, depending on their size. In a saucepan, bring the vinegars, ⅓ cup | 100 ml water and sugar to a boil. Remove from heat and add radishes. Allow to cool and refrigerate for several hours.

2. Open the scallop shells. With a soup spoon, remove the white flesh, leaving the beard and the coral in the shell. Rinse the white scallops under cold water. Allow to dry on a paper towel in the refrigerator to firm up the muscle. With a very sharp knife, slice paper-thin slices of scallops, as you would for a carpaccio. Arrange the slices attractively on 6 plates, using a plating circle if needed.

3. Dice small cubes of the slices of bread and fry until golden in a drop of oil.

...

Pairs well with
Our *Senchayamato* tea

...

Supreme the Meyer lemon (cut segments with no pith or skin) and dice finely. Make sure to save the juice. Dice the apple, leaving the skin on.

4. Whisk together the lime juice and olive oil. With a pastry brush, brush the scallops with the sauce. Dust the carpaccio lightly with the *fleur de sel* and the Espelette pepper. Sprinkle the other ingredients (croutons, diced lemon, apple cubes, radish pickles) and finish with the lime zest.

Chef's tip

When choosing scallops, make sure they are firm and are odorless. These two criteria will ensure their freshness.

THE COLORS OF
THE TEA-RAINBOW!

Green tea, blue tea, white, black and yellow tea… How do they do it?

HOW TO READ YOUR TEA-LEAVES

The secret to the tea's magnificent chromatic palette is the way tea is produced: the way the leaves are processed, and the type of oxidation they undergo.

Green teas are non-fermented, non-oxidized teas. Oxidation is stopped immediately. White teas undergo initial surface oxidation. Yellow teas are also lightly fermented like white teas but the leaves are steamed under damp cloth or straw after fermentation. They are rarer, more expensive teas with a more mellow flavor.

FERMENTED HUES

Other colors depend on the degree of fermentation. Oolong and blue teas are "semi-fermented" – oxidation is interrupted and varies between 10 and 15%–70%, giving darker fruitier beverages. Black tea involves total fermentation. Dark teas undergo accelerated fermentation, while the famous Pu Erh, undergoes post-fermentation.

Earl Grey Madeleines

Makes 30 madeleines
Preparation: 20 minutes
Cooking time: 10 minutes
Resting time: 24 hours

3 ⅓ cups | 375 g cake (SR) flour
1 cup | 200 g granulated sugar
1 ⅓ cups | 300 g butter +
3 tbsp | 40 g for the molds
4 organic eggs
⅓ cup | 90 ml milk
6 ¼ tsp | 45 g honey
4 tsp | 15 g baking powder
1 tbsp of steeped Earl Grey tea

Equipment
Stand mixer
30 Madeleine molds
Candy (sugar) thermometer

1. In the mixing bowl, whip eggs and sugar until pale and frothy. At the same time, heat the milk and honey to 140 °F | 60 °C. Sift together the flour and baking powder. Melt the butter in a small saucepan over low heat.

2. When the egg-sugar mixture is ready, slowly add the honey dissolved in the milk and combine. Add the flour mixture, tea, and melted butter. Cover and refrigerate batter for 24 hours.

3. Preheat the oven to 350 °F | 180° C | gas mark 4. Butter and lightly flour the molds. Stir the batter lightly and fill the molds. Bake the madeleines for 10 minutes.

Pairs well with
Our *Violette* tea

Fruit Salad

Serves 6 people
Preparation: 35 minutes
Resting time: 1 hour

1 ripe pineapple
1 mango
4 kiwi fruit
2 cups | 250 g strawberries
1 cup | 125 g raspberries

Syrup
½ cup | 100 g granulated sugar
½ vanilla pod
2 passion fruits

1. Slice the skin off the pineapple. Trim any remaining eyes. Cut into wedges, removing the fibrous core that is not as sweet. Cut each wedge into small triangles. Peel the mango and slice the flesh into strips. Peel the kiwi fruit. Remove the woody stem before dicing into small cubes. Quarter the strawberries. Put everything into a large salad bowl.

2. Prepare the syrup: warm ½ cup + 5 tbsp | 200 ml of water and melt the sugar. Add the sliced and scraped vanilla pod with the pulp of the passion fruits. Allow to cool.

3. Pour the syrup over the fruit. Mix gently before adding the whole raspberries. Allow to rest for 1 hour before serving.

Pairs well with
Our *Yunnan* tea

Financiers

Makes 12 financiers
Preparation: 20 minutes
Cooking time: 6–8 minutes
Resting time: minimum of 12 hours

7 tbsp | 100 g unsalted butter + 1 ½ tbsp | 20 g for molds
1 ⅛ cups | 150 g confectioners' (icing) sugar
½ cup | 50 g ground almonds (almond flour)
6 tbsp | 40 g flour
4 organic egg whites

Equipment
12 barquette or financier molds, 1.6x3.5 inches | 9x4 cm

1. In a large saucepan, melt the 7 tbsp | 100 g of butter. When the butter stops foaming, it will start to color. When the butter has turned golden brown and smells of hazelnuts, remove from heat.

2. In a large bowl, sift together the confectioners' sugar, the almond flour and the flour. Add the egg whites (do not whip them) and stir with a spatula. Add the cooled butter and mix well. Cover and refrigerate the batter for at least 12 hours.

3. The following day, preheat the oven to 410° F | 210 C | gas mark 6. Melt the remaining 1 ½ tbsp | 20 g of butter and with a small pastry brush, butter the molds. Fill the molds ¾ to the top with the batter. Place in oven and bake for 6 to 8 minutes.

4. Remove the financiers from the oven and allow to cool slightly. Remove the cakes and place on a rack to cool completely.

Pairs well with
Our *Lapsang Souchong* tea

Chef's tip

Use room temperature egg whites for a smoother batter. The batter can be kept in the refrigerator for up to 5 days if you place plastic wrap directly on the batter. You can flavor the cakes by sprinkling crushed pistachios, hazelnuts, almonds, or peanuts directly into the molds.

THE EMPEROR'S TEA TABLE

In China, some teas rule supreme. These rare "artisan" teas are created using ancestral techniques – they are the Holy Grail for tea-connoisseurs.

YELLOW TEA

In China, yellow tea is a green or white tea of such exceptional quality that it is considered supreme, a *grand cru* as it were. It is called yellow tea because *yellow* was the color of imperial power and it is a reminder of the time when each province had to surrender its finest tea harvest to the Chinese emperor.

THE LADY IN RED

Da Hong Pao (literally "big red robe") is another tea cloaked in imperial mythology. According to legend, the mother of a Ming dynasty emperor was cured of an illness by a certain tea growing on a rock on the Wuyi Mountains of the Fujian Province. The grateful emperor sent beautiful red robes to clothe the four bushes from which that tea originated. Another legend tells of how a mandarin was cured by the tea. Today there are four particular Da Hong Pao tea plants that are considered to be sacred national treasures and are guarded by the army. The majority of production is retained by the Chinese government to entertain VIPs; the other is sold at auction, at prices of up to thirty thousand dollars per ounce.

"The best quality tea must have creases like the leathern boot of Tartar horsemen, curl like the dewlap of a mighty bullock, unfold like a mist rising out of a ravine, gleam like a lake touched by a zephyr, and be wet and soft like a fine earth newly swept by rain." Lu Yu

British
TEA

...

British Tea: The National Drink

Each subject of Her Majesty the Queen drinks on average six cups of tea a day. Few nations can pride themselves on their love of tea as much as the English. And few can pride themselves on going to such measures to turn it into a lifestyle.

IT'S ALWAYS TEA O'CLOCK

In the United Kingdom, tea time is a sacred ritual: "Under certain circumstances there are few hours in life more agreeable than the hour dedicated to the ceremony known as afternoon tea." *The Portrait of a Lady*, Henry James. In Britain, tea time is as important as Sunday meals in France or Italy. It is integral to family culture and traditions.

It is a time for creature comforts, but the cakes and cookies that accompany it do not tell the whole story. The emotional attachment to tea time is no doubt rooted in childhood, but there are also hundreds of years of history related to the leaf that come into play. English culture is steeped in tea: it is to be found in nursery rhymes and Beatles tunes, the nation's great novels and its fine arts. Lewis Carroll's *Alice's Adventures in Wonderland* provides one of the most delightfully comic tea time episodes, the Mad Hatter's tea party, where the Mad Hatter, Mad March Hare and Dormouse are trapped in an eternal tea-party, because time has stopped at 6 o'clock.

LADIES FIRST!

In the wake of her coronation on 28June 1838, Queen Victoria demanded two changes at Buckingham Palace: the *Times* newspaper in the morning and tea in the afternoon. When her new routine took hold, she is said to have announced: "Now I know I truly rule." This royal afternoon tea ritual has been continued by Queen Elisabeth II. The English monarchy can thank Portugal for their delectable discovery. As part of her dowry in her marriage to King Charles II in 1662, the Portuguese princess, Catherine of Braganza, offered a chest of tea and a porcelain tea service. It is said that the first person to drink tea for breakfast was Queen Anne Stuart; but it was a duchess who introduced *five o'clock tea*. Anne, the seventh duchess of Bedford (1783–1857) is the first to have invited her friends to an afternoon collation around a cup of tea. Her idea came from the French tradition of the salon, a society gathering of notables and celebrities, which had since fallen out of fashion, but was revived in the 19th century when "Anglomania" was at its height in France.

TEA-GOWNS AND TEAROOMS

The 19th century was the heyday of afternoon tea. It was considered the height of fashion to invite one's society chums around to tea.

The 1880s saw the development of distinct tea time fashions and the tea-gown, the must-have attire for all self-respecting hostesses. Unlike the highly corseted dresses of the age, the gown allowed for freedom of movement, thanks to its sack-back and loose box pleats known as Watteau pleats, because of their appearance in paintings by the artist Antoine Watteau. Such "casual-wear" could in no instance be worn outside, but the gown met with great success in English and French high-society, and was a first, albeit small step towards the women's liberation in vestimentary matters. The spread of tearooms in the Industrial Revolution's bustling cities also afforded greater freedom to women. Like the nascent department store, tearooms were places where women were allowed to venture alone.

TEA ETIQUETTE

In Great Britain, tea has its own codified routine: from the early morning brew in bed and the post-ablutions pot of tea at the table before the day begins in earnest, to the elevenses' *cuppa* (the UK abbreviation of "cup of tea"). The conventions for the afternoon ritual are even more complex: *cream tea* (a.k.a. *Devonshire tea*) may be served with scones, clotted cream and jam, while afternoon tea is served with sandwiches, scones and a selection of cakes. High tea is different again, a meal in itself. It is the repast of the working man

after a day at the factory, involving a cooked dish, bread and butter and inevitably, tea. Where afternoon tea was a moment of indulgence and elegance at the "low-tea table", high tea was a simpler affair at the "high-tea" or dinner table. Which is why in Yorkshire you might hear the slightly surreal but very pertinent question: "Do you want tea with your tea?" The "tea-break" meanwhile was a common practice in the army and a worker's right in factories up until the 1970s.

GENTLEMEN'S TEAS

It is bad form to drink the wrong tea at the wrong time. Tea traditions are so rooted in the British character that the writer George Orwell felt the need to create his own list of eleven tea commandments in his essay "A Nice Cup of Tea" published in the *Evening Standard*, 12 January 1946: "When I look through my own recipe for the perfect cup of tea, I find no fewer than eleven outstanding points. Here are my own eleven rules, every one of which I regard as golden." He addresses all the important issues such as water temperature, the necessity for a teapot, and the milk-before or milk-after controversy. Englishmen who have travailed for the glory of tea are legion. In the 19th century there was the audacious botanist Robert Fortune who infiltrated Chinese plantations to learn the secrets of the plant from the Chinese. And there was the renowned businessman, Thomas Lipton, whose mission it was to bring tea to the masses by developing plantations in Ceylon.

Finger Sandwiches

Makes 30 sandwiches of each variety
Preparation: 15 minutes

Beaufort finger sandwiches

30 slices of wholewheat bread
20 oz | 600 g Beaufort cheese
(or other flavorful Swiss cheese)
5 tbsp | 80 g Savora mustard
(or other mild mustard)
5 tbsp | 80 ml cream

Cut the cheese into $1/6$ inch | 4 mm thick slices. Whisk the cream by hand or with a mixer and add the mustard. With a spatula, spread the mixture on all the slices of bread. Arrange the slices of cheese on half the bread and cover with the other half.
Trim the crust and cut each sandwich into two rectangles.
Wrap the sandwiches in a slightly damp dish towel and store them in the refrigerator.

Ham finger sandwiches

30 slices of white sandwich bread
1 lb 10 oz | 750 g cooked ham, sliced $1/10$ inch | 3 mm thick
1 cup | 250 g softened, unsalted butter
1 cup (4 oz) | 120 g cornichons (or gherkins)
1 pinch ground Espelette pepper (or hot Paprika)
1 pinch *fleur de sel* (or other coarse sea salt)

Cream the softened butter with the *fleur de sel* and the Espelette pepper. Slice the cornichons with a mandoline. With a spatula, spread a thin layer of butter on all the slices of bread. Arrange the pickle slices, then the ham on half the slices of bread and cover with the other half. Trim the crust and cut each sandwich into two rectangles.
Wrap the sandwiches in a slightly damp dish towel and store them in the refrigerator.

Equipment
Mandoline

30 slices of wholewheat bread
9 oz | 250 g rocket leaves
1 sprig of green basil
6 oz | 180 g aubergine
1 oz | 30 g green zucchini
1 oz | 30 g yellow zucchini
⅔ cup | 150 g ricotta
⅓ cup | 60 g grated parmesan
8 ½ tbsp | 150 ml olive oil
1 pinch ground Espelette pepper (or hot Paprika)
1 pinch *fleur de sel* (or other coarse sea salt)

Equipment
Mandoline

30 slices of squid ink bread
1 lb 5 oz | 600 g sliced, smoked salmon
3 tbsp | 45 g cream cheese
½ lime
1 pinch of Espelette pepper (or hot Paprika)
2 pinches of *fleur de sel* (or other coarse sea salt)

...

Grilled vegetable finger sandwiches

1. Process the chopped rocket, basil leaves, grated parmesan and ricotta. Clean the zucchini and aubergine. Using the mandoline, cut the vegetables into very thin slices, 1⁄10 inch | 3 mm. Salt them and brush with olive oil. Place under the grill of your oven for 4–5 minutes. Remove from the oven and set aside in a container with a little bit of olive oil.

2. With a spatula, spread a thin layer of rocket spread on all the slices of bread. Arrange the grilled vegetables on half the slices and cover with the other half. Trim the crust and cut each sandwich into two rectangles.
Wrap the sandwiches in a slightly damp dish towel and store them in the refrigerator.

Salmon finger sandwiches

Mix the cream cheese, the juice and zest of the lime, the *fleur de sel* and Espelette pepper. With a rubber spatula, spread a thin layer of the cream cheese mixture on all the slices of bread. Arrange the slices of smoked salmon on half and cover with the other half. Trim the crust and cut each sandwich into two rectangles.
Wrap the sandwiches in a slightly damp dish towel and store them in the refrigerator.

Chicken finger sandwiches

30 slices of white bread
1 lb 10 oz | 750 g cooked
chicken breast
2 ⅔ tbsp | 30 g grated parmesan
6 organic eggs
1 pinch ground Espelette pepper
(or hot Paprika)
1 pinch *fleur de sel* (or other
coarse sea salt)

Caesar dressing (½ cup | 120 g)
1 organic egg
1 organic egg yolk
¾ tbsp | 10 g grated parmesan
5 tbsp | 70 ml grape seed oil
Freshly squeezed juice from
a ¼ of a lemon
3 anchovy filets (packed in olive oil)
1 tsp | 5 ml sherry vinegar
1 drop of Tabasco
2 drops Worcestershire sauce
2 tbsp of plain, low fat yogurt
2 pinches of table salt

1. Prepare the Caesar dressing: boil the egg and shell once cooled. Mix the raw egg yolk with the hard-boiled egg and the parmesan. Whisk the mixture with a few drops of grape seed oil to start a mayonnaise. Add the drained anchovies and mix well. Continue to add the oil slowly to finish the mayonnaise. Add the lemon juice, Tabasco, the Worcestershire, sherry vinegar, drained low-fat yogurt and salt.

2. Boil the 6 eggs. Shell and chop them. Mix the Caesar dressing with the chopped eggs and the parmesan. Cut the chicken breasts in thin slices. With a rubber spatula, spread the Caesar salad on all the slices of bread. Arrange the slices of chicken on half and cover with the other half. Trim the crust and cut each sandwich into two rectangles. Wrap the sandwiches in a slightly damp dish towel and store them in the refrigerator.

Pairs well with
Our *Ceylan* tea

Ladurée Club Sandwich

Serves 6 people
Preparation: 40 minutes
Cooking time: 10 minutes
Drying time: 6–8 minutes

1 lb | 480 g cooked chicken breasts
12 slices of white bread
6 organic eggs
6 slices of pastrami
3 tomatoes
1 lettuce heart
1 package of red shiso microgreens
1 pinch of table salt

Mayonnaise (1 ⅓ cups | 300 g)
3 organic egg yolks
2 tbsp | 30 g Dijon mustard
1 cup | 250 ml vegetable oil
1 splash of white vinegar
1 pinch of ground Espelette pepper
(or hot Paprika)
1 pinch of salt

Equipment
Wooden skewers

1. Bring a pot of water to boil and carefully add eggs. Cook for 10 minutes. Run under cold water before shelling.

2. Cut the chicken breasts into slices. Wash the tomatoes and cut into thin slices along with the hard-boiled eggs.

3. Prepare the mayonnaise: put the egg yolks in a bowl with rounded edges and just big enough to hold the desired quantity of mayonnaise. Add the mustard, salt and Espelette pepper. Whisk until all the ingredients are fully incorporated. Slowly pour a slow stream of oil while continuing to whisk briskly. Add the vinegar and season to taste. Place in the refrigerator.

• • •

4. Prepare the pastrami crisps: preheat the oven to 350°F | 180°C | gas mark 4. Cut each thin slice of pastrami in half and dry between 2 baking sheets for 6 to 8 minutes.

5. Wash and dry the salad. Chop the leaves finely and add them to the mayonnaise.

6. Assemble the club sandwiches. Toast 2 slices of bread. Spread some of the mayonnaise-lettuce mixture on 1 slice. Garnish with egg, tomato, a slice of chicken and another spoon of the mayonnaise-lettuce mixture. Cover with the second slice of toast and press firmly. Skewer the sandwich all the way through to hold it together. With a bread knife, trim the crusts.

7. Cut the sandwich into 3 identical rectangles and arrange on a plate. Finish plating with 2 pastrami crisps and several shiso microgreens. Repeat for the 5 other club sandwiches.

Pairs well with
Our *Darjeeling* tea

THE ART OF BLENDING

The English are masters of blending tea, an art that dates back to colonial times.

VIP RECIPES

English Breakfast Tea is an English blend composed of Ceylon, Assam and Kenyan teas, made popular by Queen Victoria. Today it is the tea most consumed in the world. The Prince of Wales tea blend is named after Prince Edward who in 1921 gave Twinings his royal seal of approval to market his own personal blend – a combination of Chinese black teas and Keemun teas from the Anhui Province in China. Unlike other blends, the recipe isn't set in stone and sometimes Ceylon and Assam teas are used as well as blackcurrant aromas.

FIFTY SHADES OF EARL GREY

The great English classic, Earl Grey, is a blend of Chinese, Darjeeling, and Ceylon tea with a hint of Lapsang Souchong flavored with bergamot orange. It owes its name to Earl Charles Grey, the British Prime Minister from 1830 to 1834. According to one legend, a grateful Chinese mandarin – whose son was rescued from drowning by one of Earl Grey's men – first presented the blend to the Earl in 1803. It seems however that Earl Grey never set foot in China. It is more likely that he simply added a slice of bergamot orange to his tea one day. Fiction is generally less prosaic than reality. Two companies, Jacksons of Piccadilly and Twinings, also claim to have created the drink.

Mimosa Eggs

Serves 6 people
Preparation: 30 minutes
Cooking time: 15 minutes
Drying time: 15–20 minutes

15 organic eggs
2 oz | 60 g pastrami
½ oz | 12 g salmon roe
½ cup | 120 g mayonnaise
1 bunch of chives
3 tbsp | 30 g brown flax seeds
3 tbsp | 30 g golden flax seeds
2 ⅔ tbsp | 60 g grated parmesan
1 drop olive oil
Salt, pepper

Salmon Rillettes
1 ½ oz | 40 g raw salmon (certified sea-raised salmon)
1 oz | 25 g sliced smoked salmon
2 tsp | 10 g cream cheese
10 sprigs of chives
Juice of ½ a lemon

1. Bring a pot of water to boil and carefully add eggs. Cook for 10 minutes and run under cold water before shelling.

2. Prepare the salmon rillettes: slice the raw salmon into small pavés and steam at 203°F | 95°C for 10 minutes. Place in refrigerator.

3. Meanwhile, trim the smoked salmon of dark portions and cut into small cubes. Wash and mince the chives. Whip the cream and add the lemon juice and fleur de sel.

4. When the salmon is cold, mash it with a fork and add the smoked salmon, the chives, the cream cheese and the lemon juice. Add olive oil and Espelette pepper. Mix thoroughly to achieve a homogenous spread. Adjust seasoning to taste.

⅓ cup | 100 ml heavy (double) cream
1 dash of organic olive oil
1 pinch of Espelette pepper
(or hot Paprika)
1 pinch of *fleur de sel* (or other coarse sea salt)

Mushroom duxelles

⅔ cup | 40 g button mushrooms
¾ cup | 190 ml heavy (double) cream
5 tsp | 25 g unsalted butter
1 pinch of Espelette pepper
(or hot Paprika)
1 pinch table salt

Equipment

Piping bag fitted with a plain tip, ⅙ inch | 4 mm diameter

•••

5. Prepare the duxelles: clean the mushrooms, cut any dirty stems and quickly rinse. Dice finely, including the stems. Heat the butter in a saucepan, taking care to not let it brown. Add the mushrooms and cook over a low flame, stirring occasionally with a wooden spatula until all of the liquid has evaporated. Season.

6. Cut the hard-boiled eggs in half lengthwise. Remove the yolks, taking care not to damage the whites. Put the yolks in a *cul-de-poule* (hemispherical bowl). Cream the yolks with a fork. Add the mayonnaise and chives and mix again. Season to taste. Place the mimosa cream into the piping bag fitted with its tip.

7. Preheat the oven to 325°F | 160°C | gas mark 3 for 8 minutes. Dry the pastrami between 2 baking sheets for 15–20 minutes. Crumble the resulting crisps. Next, prepare the parmesan crisps. Spread the grated parmesan on a baking sheet and place in the oven for 6 minutes. Take the parmesan crisps out of the oven and crumble them as well.

•••

8. In a frying pan, roast the flax seeds in a drop of olive oil. The seeds will puff.

9. Fill the egg whites with the mimosa cream. Garnish each with a different topping: pastrami, parmesan, salmon roe, or puffed seeds. Sprinkle the minced chives over all of them.

Pairs well with
Our *Breakfast* tea

Viennese Shortbread

Makes 40 shortbread biscuits
Preparation: 30 minutes
Cooking time: 15–20 minutes

1 ½ cup + 5 ½ tbsp | 350 g butter + 1 ½ tbsp | 20 g for baking sheet
1 pinch of *fleur de sel* (or other coarse sea salt)
⅔ cup | 75 g confectioners' (icing) sugar
1 pinch of powdered vanilla (or a few drops of vanilla extract)
1 organic egg white
1 ¾ cup | 225 g cake (SR) flour

Equipment
Piping bag fitted with a ⅙ inch | 4 mm star tip

1. Cut the butter into small pieces. Put butter and *fleur de sel* in a heatproof bowl set over a pan of gently simmering water. Using a wooden spoon, beat until soft and creamy.
Remove from heat and whisk until smooth.
Add the following ingredients, one after the other, making sure to mix well after each addition: confectioners' sugar, powdered vanilla and the egg white. Whisk together.

2. Preheat the oven to 300 °F | 150 °C | gas mark 2. Sift flour into the previous mixture and stir with a wooden spoon until smooth.

3. Immediately transfer batter to piping bag fitted with a star tip. Butter a baking sheet or line with parchment paper, and pipe spiral discs with a diameter of 2 inches | 6 cm. Bake for 15–20 minutes until the shortbread is golden.
Allow to cool completely. Store in an airtight container in a cool, dry place.

Pairs well with
Our *Violette* tea

Chocolate Orange Cake

Serves 8 to 10 people
Preparation: 1 ½ hours
Cooking time: 55 minutes
Resting time: minimum of 12 hours

Poached orange slices
1 orange
¾ cup + 2 tbsp | 200 ml water
½ cup | 100 g granulated sugar

Chocolate cake batter
½ cup | 75 g golden seedless raisins (sultanas)
10 ½ tbsp | 150 g butter +
1 tbsp | 15 g for loaf pan
1 cup | 130 g all-purpose flour (reserve 1 tbsp | 10 g for loaf pan)
⅓ cup | 30 g unsweetened cocoa powder
1 ½ tsp | ½ packet | 5 ½ g baking powder
¾ cup | 150 g granulated sugar
3 organic eggs
1 ¼ cups | 210 g diced candied orange peel

POACHED ORANGE SLICES AND RAISINS
The day before:
1. Cut the orange into thin ⅒ inch | 2 mm slices. Bring water and sugar to a simmer and carefully add the orange slices. Poach over low heat for 30 minutes without allowing the liquid to boil. Allow to cool. Gently drain the oranges slices and keep in refrigerator.

2. Place raisins in a bowl and pour hot water to cover them by ⅓ inch | 1 cm. Cover the bowl with plastic wrap and leave them to swell for a minimum of 12 hours at room temperature. Drain thoroughly.

CHOCOLATE CAKE BATTER
3. Butter the loaf pan and line with a long rectangle of parchment paper to make unmolding easier.

Orange syrup

⅔ cup | 150 ml orange juice
½ cup + 2 tbsp | 120 g granulated sugar
⅓ cup | 80 ml Grand Marnier

Orange glaze

2 oz | 50 g orange jelly
1 tbsp | 115ml water

Equipment

Loaf pan, 10 x 3 x 3 inch | 25 x 8 x 8 cm

Refrigerate for 10 minutes to allow the butter to harden. Remove from refrigerator and dust the interior with flour. Turn upside down and lightly tap out any excess flour.

4. Bring butter and eggs to room temperature. In a bowl, sift together the cocoa powder, flour and baking powder. In a second bowl, work the butter until creamy. Add the sugar and whisk vigorously. Continue to whisk and add the eggs one at a time. Using a wooden or rubber spatula, fold in the cocoa mixture. Add the drained raisins and diced candied orange peel.

5. Preheat the oven to 425 °F | 220 °C | gas mark 7. Fill the loaf pan with batter to ¾-inch | 2-cm below the rim. Place in oven and bake for 10 minutes. Remove from oven and with a sharp knife, slit the crust lengthwise. Immediately return the cake to the oven and lower the temperature to 350 °F | 180 °C | gas mark 4. Bake for 40 to 45 minutes. Check to see if the cake is done by inserting the tip of a knife into the center. When the cake is ready, the knife should come out clean, dry, and free of crumbs.

ORANGE SYRUP

6. While the cake is baking, prepare the syrup. Bring orange juice and sugar to a boil. Remove from heat and pour in the Grand Marnier.

7. Place a cooling rack on a rimmed baking sheet. When the cake is done, remove from the pan and place on the rack. Bring the syrup back to a simmer. Using a ladle, pour syrup over cake and allow it to soak in. Gather syrup from baking sheet and pour over cake. Repeat twice. Allow to cool. Decorate the top of the cake with the poached orange slices.

ORANGE GLAZE
8. Gently heat the orange jelly and water in a saucepan (approximately 122 °F to 140 °F | 50 °C to 60 °C), making sure it does not come to a boil. Cook until the mixture is thick enough to coat the back of a spoon.
Coat the cake with glaze.

Pairs well with
Our *Ceylan* tea

MAKE THE GRADE!

The tea grading system is based on two factors: the type of harvest and the size of leaves.

WHOLE LEAVES

There are several grades of whole leaves: Pekoe (P), a word which refers to the down-like white "hairs" on the leaf and also to the youngest leaf buds. Souchong (S), two leaves and the end shoot. Orange Pekoe, several leaves and the leaf shoot; Flowery Orange Pekoe (FOP), the young bud with two leaves; Flowery Pekoe (FP), a coarser, fleshier leaf. Indian grades are: Golden Flowery Orange Pekoe (GFOP), a grade equivalent to FOP but with golden tips; Tippy Golden Flowery Orange Pekoe (TGFOP), with only golden tips; and the highest grades, Finest Tippy Golden Flowery Orange Pekoe (FTGFOP) and Special Finest Tippy Golden Flowery Orange Pekoe (SFTGFOP).

BROKEN LEAVES

The same system applies but a B for "broken" is added: Broken Pekoe Souchong (BPS), Broken Orange Pekoe (BOP), Finest Broken Orange Pekoe (FBOP), Golden Broken Orange Pekoe (GBOP), Golden Flowery Broken Orange Pekoe (GFBOP) and Tippy Golden Broken Orange Pekoe (TGBOP). There are also the finer tea particles: "fannings" (F), flecks of tea smaller than broken leaves and "dust" (D) – again the letters are combined with the P, O, GO, F, BOP, OP classifications above.

Lime and Coconut Tarts

Serves 8 people
Preparation: 1 hour and 15 minutes
+ Basic Recipes, p. 300
Cooking time: 35 minutes
Refrigeration time: 13 hours
Freezer time: 1 hour

Lime cream
1 lime, unwaxed
¾ cup + 2 tbsp | 170 g granulated sugar
2 tbsp | 5 g cornstarch (cornflour)
3 organic eggs
½ cup | 115 ml of lime juice
1 cup + 1 ½ tbsp | 250 g butter

Coconut cream
¼ cup | 60 ml heavy (double) cream
2 tbsp | 25 g butter
3 tbsp | 25 g confectioners' (icing) sugar
2 tbsp | 25 g shredded coconut
1 tbsp of dark rum (rhum agricole if possible)
1 organic egg
3 tbsp | 25 g cornstarch (cornflour)

The day before, prepare the lime cream and almond pastry dough (see recipe p. 297).

LIME CREAM

1. Using a grater, zest the lime. In a bowl, mix together the sugar and grated zest. Add the cornstarch, the eggs one at a time, and the lime juice.
In a saucepan, cook the mixture over low heat, stirring with a spatula until it simmers, allowing the cream to thicken. Remove from heat.
Leave for 10 minutes to cool slightly. The cream should be hot but not scalding (approximately 140 °F | 60 °C). Add the softened butter.
In a blender or food processor, blend the butter into the lime cream until perfectly smooth.
Pour into an airtight container and refrigerate for at least 12 hours until firm.

...

Sweet almond pastry shells
12 ½ oz | 350 g dough: see
Basic Recipe, p.297
3 tbsp flour for work surface
1 ½ tbsp | 20 g butter for tartlet pans

Lime Glaze
2 oz | 50 g lime jelly (jam)
1 tbsp water
Grated zest of limes and candied limes for decoration

Equipment
8 tartlet pans, 3 inch | 8 cm diameter and ¾ inch | 2 cm high
Cookie cutter 4 ½ inch | 12-cm diameter
Candy (sugar) thermometer

COCONUT CREAM
2. The following day, place a large mixing bowl into the freezer to chill. Pour the cold heavy cream into the chilled bowl and whip energetically until firm. In another bowl, mix the softened butter along with the confectioners' sugar and coconut. Add the rum, egg and cornstarch. Incorporate the whipped cream.

SWEET ALMOND PASTRY SHELLS
3. Butter the tartlet pans. On a floured work surface, roll out the dough to ⅟₁₀ inch | 2 mm thick. Using a round pastry cutter or a small bowl, cut out 8 disks that are approximately 5 inches | 12 cm in diameter and press into buttered pans. Allow to rest in the refrigerator for 1 hour.

4. Preheat the oven to 325 °F | 165 °C | gas mark 3. Remove the tartlet shells from the refrigerator. Using a fork, prick the surface of the dough to avoid distortions during baking. Fit a round piece of parchment paper over the dough, carefully pressing into the corners and working up the sides so it will stay in place in the oven.
Place dried beans or pie weights on top, spreading them out in an even layer.
Bake for approximately 15 minutes until lightly colored. Remove from oven.

• • •

5. Allow to cool slightly before removing dried beans and parchment paper.
Immediately fill with a thin layer of coconut cream (1/10–1/8 inch | 2–3 mm thick).
Return to hot oven and bake for approximately 10 minutes for the pastry and cream to color.
Remove from oven, unmold and allow to cool.

6. Spoon the lime cream into the baked tartlet shells, fill to the top of the pastry and smooth the surface with a metal spatula. Freeze to chill the top of the cream (approximately 1 hour).

LIME GLAZE

7. In a saucepan, stir together the lime jelly and 1 tbsp water over low heat. Cook without boiling (approximately 122–140°F | 50–60 °C) until it coats the back of a spoon. Remove the tartlets from freezer and with a pastry brush, coat with glaze. Decorate with grated lime zest as seen in the photo.

Pairs well with
Our *Earl Grey* tea

A SPOT OF MILK?

The British are famously fond of adding milk to their breakfast or afternoon tea to soften the bitter tannins.

MADE IN FRANCE

Tea purists would advise drinking their *cuppa* unadulterated by milk, lemon or sugar. It is said that the idea of adding milk came from France. Eager to protect their delicate porcelain tea services, ladies of the nobility would insist on pouring cold milk into their cups to prevent them cracking when the hot tea hit the delicate porcelain. Proud of their dairy production, the English adopted the habit and it has stuck ever since.

THE TEA OF HUMAN KINDNESS

According to recent medical research, the addition of milk negates tea's beneficial effects on our arteries. The polyphenols in tea prevent the hardening of the arteries and encourage blood circulation. In 2017 however, Doctor Verena Stangl and her cardiology team in Berlin showed that casein in milk blocks the action of polyphenols. Their research could help explain why big tea drinking nations such as Great Britain do not benefit from the same positive effects of tea as Asian countries where tea is drunk pure.

TEA and Brunch

...

Photographs produced at the Ladurée Geneva Tearoom, decorated by India Mahdavi.

Tea and Brunch

Tea time is anytime – don't tie yourself down. New trends in cooking have made tea the drink for every hour of the day – especially at brunch.

AN ANGLO-SAXON TIC

"Brunch" – the cunning linguistic contraction of breakfast and lunch- first became popular in the 19th century among hunters who would enjoy a light meal of cold meats, pies and sweetmeats on returning from their morning's hunt. Today brunch is a festive friends-and-family affair – brunching solo can feel lonely, albeit a deliciously self-indulgent pleasure. France only began to brunch in the 1990s. Across the globe different cultures offer local variations on the theme. In the United States, the menu differs from state to state. Today, brunch is the perfect Sunday pick-me-up after a late night out and in New York, fruit-juice cocktails are de rigueur, a theme that dates back to Prohibition era when Harry's Bar relocated to Paris and its owner dreamed up the Bloody Mary as the perfect "hair-of-the dog".

FESTIVE AND REGRESSIVE

Brunch is generally served as a buffet, whether at home or in restaurants. The sweet and savory combination seems to scorn traditional protocols of when to eat what. Anything goes. It is a moment of comfort-eating among familiars – the perfect time to chew the fat and sip tea. The menu is limited only by your imagination. It generally incorporates teas, fruit juice, fruit, coffee, hot chocolate, pastries, toast, pancakes, muffins, cakes and savory dishes such as scrambled eggs, eggs benedict, bacon, sausages, chicken, cheese, salad and quiches. Smoked teas, Breakfast Tea or Earl Grey, are the perfect pairing. You might also opt for a stronger Yunnan, a tonic Ceylon with its woody notes, or a Jasmine tea from China. Hence brunch offers the ideal opportunity to indulge in savory fare while drinking tea, an art of living that the Far East has enjoyed for centuries.

ALL THE TEA IN CHINA

In China and Japan, tea is drunk with every meal, at all times of the day, as well as in the evening, due to its digestive and hydrating properties. The toasted notes of roasted Japanese green teas work well with savory dishes and the marine notes of green teas are marvelous with raw fish. The Chinese have their own brunch: *dim sum*, a meal that spans from the morning throughout the afternoon. It has its roots in the ancient tradition of *yum cha* (literally "drink tea") where the focus is on the combination of food and tea. As traders traveled the Silk Road, teahouses sprung up along the way offering a place to rest and eat *dim sum*, snack-size portions of fried and steamed, sweet and savory dumplings served in bamboo steamers from a cart. The choice of tea is of vital importance and unlimited hot water is served on tables in the same way as carafes of tap water are served elsewhere.

SAVORY PAIRINGS

Europe has also begun to wake up to the aromatic wonders of tea and the possibilities for daring and delicious pairings with food. In the past ten years, chefs across the continent have experimented with new forms of cuisine to accompany the leaf. Tea has become the new wine and, not only chefs, but oenologists have also become fascinated by its potential. Its expansive aromatic palette makes for a vast array of combinations. And for those averse to lunch-time drinking, it provides a perfect gastronomic alternative. The Michelin-starred chef Alain Passard is one such aficionado. In his Parisian restaurant *l'Arpège*, Passard is reluctant to serve fish with chilled white wine because in his opinion, white wine actually impairs its flavor as its cold acidity congeals fish oils on the taste buds: fish is better complemented with the lighter fresher notes of green tea.

Tea is generally gentler and unassuming; it doesn't overpower the palate, which means flavors can develop without competing, making it an excellent aromatic accompaniment for all dishes.

Avocado Toast
(brioche, avocado & scrambled eggs)

Serves 6 people
Preparation: 20 minutes
Cooking time: 15 minutes

1 brioche (mousseline)
2 avocados
½ bunch of coriander
1 lime
3 ½ oz | 100 g roasted bell peppers marinated in oil
1 pinch of ground Espelette pepper (or hot Paprika)
1 pinch of salt

Scrambled eggs
6 organic eggs
⅓ cup | 100 ml heavy (double) cream
3 ½ tbsp | 50 g "extrafin" butter (butter made from fresh cream that has never been frozen)
Salt

Garnish
36 pumpkin seeds
1 punnet of micro-coriander
Fleur de sel (or other coarse sea salt)

1. Cut the avocados in half, remove the pits and scoop out the flesh. With a fork, mash the avocado. Mince the roasted bell peppers and coriander. Mix all the ingredients and season with the zest and juice of the lime, the Espelette pepper and salt. Set aside.

2. Prepare the scrambled eggs: Crack the eggs into a bowl and add the salt. Gently whisk the eggs until the mixture starts to froth. Melt the butter in saucepan. Add the eggs and cook over a low flame, stirring constantly, until the eggs are cooked to your liking. Add the cream to stop the eggs from overcooking and remove from heat.

3. Cut the brioche into ½ inch | 1 ½ cm thick slices.

...

Pairs well with
Our *Jardin Bleu Royal* tea

4. Preheat the oven to a low broil. Spread the pumpkin seeds out on a baking sheet. Broil them for 5 minutes, making sure to stir them regularly until they are all golden.

5. Place the slices of brioche on a baking sheet and place in the oven (still on broil) for 3 to 4 minutes, turning them over at the half way mark in order to toast both sides.

6. Place 1 slice of brioche on a plate and spread the avocado-roasted pepper mixture over it. Layer the scrambled eggs on top. Decorate the plate with the toasted pumpkin seeds, *fleur de sel* and coriander microgreens.

Chef's tip

Choose organic eggs if possible. Eggs produced in the EU are required to have a code stamped on their shells. Organic eggs start with "0", followed by the abbreviation of their country of origin. This code helps trace the egg and states how the hens were raised.

PAIRING TEA WITH FOOD

Tea tasting and choosing the right tea for the right food is an art. It even has its own dedicated profession these days: tea sommelier.

ALL IN THE SENSES
Even if you're not looking to change your day-job, the basics of tasting are within everyone's reach. Tea tasting is about a sensual experience and focusing on the aromas and flavors of the beverage, in the same way as wine. With concentration and experience, you'll soon build up your own mental repertoire of flavors and fragrances for reference.

TWO TYPES OF PAIRING
When it comes to pairing tea with food, two types of association are possible. Plan A: Go with the flow. Find simple harmonies in similar flavors: the citrus notes of bergamot and Earl Grey combine brilliantly with lemon desserts; magnolia-scented green and black teas from China provide the light and delicate notes required for financiers; among savory dishes, smoky Lapsang Souchong is perfect with cooked meats and salmon. Or plan B: Work with contrasts. Roasted, woody notes provide a delectable context for the buttery sweetness of pastries; Yunnan tea with its tobacco and malt undertones are a hit with brioche and puff pastry; floral Jasmine tea is a succulent companion for dense cocoa flavors; while spiced Indian tea with its cinnamon and cardamom notes works wonders with chicken or pork.

Ladurée Omelette

Serves 6 people
Preparation: 30 minutes
Cooking time: 30 minutes

18 organic eggs
¾ cup | 200 ml heavy (double) cream
4 oz | 120 g boiled ham
½ cup + 5 tbsp | 100 g grated Swiss cheese
4 cups | 250 g button mushrooms
4 tomatoes
1 large white onion
1 sprig of thyme
2 tbsp | 30 g unsalted butter
10 sprigs of chives
2 sprigs of chervil
2 sprigs of flat leaf parsley
Salt

Clarified butter
7 tbsp | 100 g unsalted butter

1. Start by clarifying the butter. In a small saucepan, melt the butter over very low heat until it liquefies. Remove from heat and allow the butter to separate. Filter through a clean cloth or a fine mesh sieve. Store in the refrigerator.

2. Prepare the omelette batter. Whisk the eggs with the cream. Add salt.

3. Prepare the filling: peel, wash and cook the mushrooms with butter. Dice the cooked ham.

4. Peel, seed and dice the tomatoes. Mince the onion and sweat it in butter. Add the diced tomatoes and a sprig of thyme. Season lightly. Allow the mushrooms and tomatoes to cook down until dry. Remove the thyme and adjust seasoning.

• • •

Garnish
1 tomato
Several chervil leaves
Fleur de sel (or other coarse sea salt)

5. Mix together the tomatoes, mushrooms (save a few for the final garnish) and the diced ham. Keep the filling warm. Chop the herbs.

6. Heat a non-stick pan. If needed, add a drizzle of clarified butter and pour in 100 ml of egg batter. Allow to cook over low heat for 2 to 3 minutes depending on if you prefer a wet or dry omelette. Fill with grated cheese, mushroom and tomato filling and a pinch of herbs. Roll the omelette onto a plate. To roll it cleanly, slide it to the edge opposite the handle. Fold the outside third to the middle. With your wrist, give a shake to the frying pan and finish rolling the omelette out of the pan and onto the plate.
Repeat the steps for the 5 other omelettes.

7. With a pastry brush, paint the top of the omelette with clarified butter. Add a spoonful of the mushroom-tomato filling to the top to garnish. Decorate with a few chervil leaves and a sprinkle of *fleur de sel*. Serve immediately.

Pairs well with
Our *Earl Grey* tea

THE IDEAL INGREDIENT

Don't throw away your left-over tea-leaves, recycle them and get cooking!

SWEET TEA
The flavor of tea in desserts is nothing new: Earl Grey jelly and Matcha cookies and fruit cakes are already familiar fare. Ceylon tea adds a delightful touch to a rum baba, while strawberries and raspberries steeped in rose tea make for a sophisticated fruit salad. Several years ago, Europe turned green when it discovered the joy of Japanese Matcha and began to incorporate it into traditional baking recipes, creating sponges, madeleines and financiers etc. Chantilly cream in a delightful shade of Matcha never fails to delight.

SAVORY TEA
Tea is gradually making its way into savory recipes too. Its subtle undertones make for surprising variations on familiar favorites. Lapsang Souchong provides a delicious enhancement for oven-baked salmon while chicken breasts find an unusual pan-partner with astringent Chinese green teas. Dried beans and pulses, especially lentils, discover a whole new personality when cooked in spiced tea.

Ladurée Granola

Serves 6 people
Preparation: 30 minutes
Cooking time: 10 minutes

1 ½ cups + 2 tbsp | 190 g oatmeal
1 ½ cups + 2 tbsp | 40 g puffed rice
6 ½ tbsp | 60 g dark brown sugar
6 tbsp | 30 g shredded coconut
4 tbsp | 40 g unblanched almonds
3 tbsp | 35 g blanched hazelnuts
4 ½ tbsp | 35 g shelled walnuts
3 tbsp + ¾ tsp | 70 ml maple syrup
1 ½ oz | 40 g dark chocolate (milk chocolate for a sweeter flavor)
¼ tsp | 1 g *fleur de sel* (or other coarse sea salt)

1. In a large bowl, mix the dark brown sugar, the oatmeal, the shredded coconut, the puffed rice and the *fleur de sel*.

2. Preheat the oven to 325 °F | 165 °C | gas mark 3. Spread the nuts on a baking tray and roast until the hazelnuts are golden through to the middle. This should take approximately 10 minutes. Chop the nuts and add to the first mixture.

3. Pour the maple syrup on the mixture and stir carefully so as not to crumble the oatmeal. Spread the granola on the baking sheet and let it dry at 300 °F | 150 °C | gas mark 2 for 10 minutes. Do not leave the granola in the oven for too long because the maple syrup will caramelize and the nuts will start to burn.

4. Remove from oven and allow to cool completely. Add the chopped chocolate. You can also replace the chocolate with chopped, dried fruit.

Pairs well with
Our *Jardin Bleu Royal* tea

Brioche

Makes 1 brioche
Preparation: 1 ½ hours
Resting time: 6–7 hours
Cooking time: 30 minutes

1 cup + 6 ½ tbsp | 175 g flour +
2 ½ tbsp | 20 g flour for work surface
2 tbsp | 25 g granulated sugar
2 tsp | 6 g fresh yeast
½ cup | 115 g butter +
2 tbsp | 30 g for the mold
3 organic eggs + 1 organic egg for the glaze
2 tbsp | 3 g salt

Equipment
Non-stick brioche mold,
8 inch | 20 cm in diameter

Ideally, the dough should be prepared 10 hours before baking time.

1. Place the flour in a large bowl. Add the sugar and salt on one side of the flour. Crumble the fresh yeast with your fingers and place on the other side. Important: the yeast must not come in contact with the sugar and salt before you start to mix the dough; otherwise it will lose its strength.

2. Cut the butter into small pieces.
In a bowl, whisk the eggs. Pour ⅔ of the eggs over the flour and begin by mixing all ingredients together with a wooden spatula. Incorporate the remaining third of the eggs little by little. Knead the dough with your hands, until it starts to pull away from the sides of the bowl. Add the butter and continue to work the dough until it once again pulls away from the sides of the bowl.

3. Transfer the dough to a large, clean bowl and cover with a damp dish towel or plastic wrap and keep at room temperature. Allow the dough to double in volume (approximately 2 ½ hours).

...

Return the dough to its initial volume by folding it back on itself. Refrigerate for 2 ½ hours.
The dough will rise again while chilling. Knock it back again by folding it back on itself. The dough is ready to be used.

4. On a floured work surface, divide the dough into two; one portion should weigh 5 oz | 150 g and the other 15 oz | 450 g. Using the palm of your hand, flatten each portion and fold it back over itself into a tight ball.

5. Rub a piece of butter all over the inside of the mold. Place the larger ball inside the mold, with the fold underneath. With your finger, open a hole on top. Shape the smaller ball into a cone and place inside the hole.
Allow the dough to rise again for 1 to 2 hours depending on the warmth of your kitchen (ideally, it should be warm and humid).

6. Preheat the oven to 325 °F | 160° C | gas mark 4. With a pastry brush, paint the top of the brioche lightly with the beaten egg. With a pair of scissors, cut 5 snips ($^3/_4$-inch | 2-cm deep) between the head and the edge of the mold, evenly spaced all the way around. Lower oven to 340 °F | 170 °F | gas mark 3 and carefully place the brioche inside. Allow to bake for 30 minutes. Remove from oven and allow the brioche to dry for 5 minutes before unmolding.

Pairs well with
Our *Amande* or *Jasmin* tea

Custard Tart

Serves 8 people

Preparation: 1 hour + Basic Recipe: 20 minutes

Cooking time: approximately 45 minutes

Resting time: 1 hour + Basic Recipe: minimum of 2 hours, preferably 12 hours

Shortcrust pastry shell
See recipe p. 296
2 ½ tbsp | 20 g flour for work surface
1 ½ tbsp | 20 g butter for the pan

Custard filling
1 vanilla pod
2 cups + 2 tbsp | 500 ml whole milk
1 ⅓ cups | 325 ml heavy (double) cream
2 organic eggs + 2 yolks
1 cup + 1 tbsp | 210 g granulated sugar
⅔ cup | 85 g cornstarch (cornflour)
2 tbsp | 25 g butter

SHORTCRUST PASTRY SHELL

1. Prepare the shortcrust pastry shell as indicated on p. 296.
On a floured work surface, roll the dough out to a thickness of ⅒ inch | 2 mm.
Butter the tart pan and gently press the dough into the pan and work up the sides. Refrigerate for at least an hour.

CUSTARD FILLING

2. With a sharp knife, slice the vanilla pod in half lengthwise. Using the tip, scrape the interior to remove the seeds. Pour the milk and cream into a saucepan. Add the vanilla pod and seeds. Bring to a simmer. Remove from heat, cover and leave to infuse for 15 minutes. Remove the pods and set aside.

Equipment
Tart pan, 9 inch | 22 ½ cm diameter, 1 ¼ inches | 3 cm high

3. Preheat the oven to 325° F | 165 °C | gas mark 3. Using a fork, prick the surface of the dough to keep it from distorting during baking. Fit a round piece of parchment paper over the dough, carefully pressing into the corners and working up the sides so it will stay in place in the oven.
Place dried beans or pie weights on top, spreading them out in an even layer. Bake for approximately 20 minutes until slightly golden.
Remove from oven. Allow to cool slightly before removing dried beans and parchment paper.

4. In a large bowl, whisk the eggs, yolks and sugar until the mixture pales slightly. Add the cornstarch. In a saucepan, bring the vanilla-infused milk to a simmer. Pour ⅓ of the hot liquid over the yolk, sugar and cornstarch mixture. Whisk together and pour back into the saucepan with the rest of the cream and milk. Bring to a boil while continuing to stir, making sure to scrape down the sides of the pan. Remove from heat, pour the custard into a large bowl and allow to cool slightly for approximately 10 minutes.

5. Meanwhile, preheat the oven to 325 °F | 165 °C | gas mark 3. While the custard is still hot but not scalding, add the butter and stir until smooth. Pour the custard into the pre-baked tart shell. Place in oven and bake for approximately 45 minutes.

Pairs well with
Our *Mélange Ladurée* tea

EVERY TEA HAS ITS TIME

Tea can be drunk from morning till night. Different teas bring different benefits and different levels of theine – the name for caffeine found in tea.

MORNING AND LUNCH
For a great start to the day, you should begin with invigorating black teas such as Darjeeling, English Breakfast or Ceylon, which are strong in theine.
A number of teas make for perfect lunch time companions; smoky Lapsang Souchong, Japanese green teas with marine notes and Jasmine tea.

AFTERNOON AND EVENING
Snack-times demand zest and tang. Opt for full and flavorsome Chinese and Ceylon blends with floral fragrances, Chinese green teas with ginger, rose and orange water, Chinese black tea with citrus fruits or the classic Earl Grey.
In the evening, there are several varieties of low-theine teas to choose from: Yunnan, Chinese black tea with its beautiful long leaf, Pu Erh tea with its digestive benefits or the blue teas of Oolong, which can be drunk throughout the evening, alone or with a light meal.

Royal TEA

...

Royal Tea

Aristocracies around the world developed their own art of living around tea, based on the French style of ornate parlors, regal porcelain, elegant silverware and stately tearooms.

THE MIRACLE ELIXIR

When tea was introduced to Britain, it was advertised as a medicine. Thomas Garraway, owner of Garraway's coffee house in London, claimed that tea would, "maketh the body active and lusty" but also "…removeth the obstructions of the spleen…" and that it was "very good against the Stone and Gravel, cleaning the Kidneys and Uriters." The Dutch doctor Cornelius Decker, profusely prescribed the consumption of tea, recommending eight to ten cups per day and claiming to drink 50–100 cups daily himself. Samuel Johnson was yet another doctor known to indulge in excessive tea drinking, rumored to have consumed as many as sixteen cups at one tea party and was an avid defender of the health benefits of tea. In 1730, Thomas Short performed many experiments on the health effects of tea and published the results, claiming that it had curative properties against ailments such as scurvy, indigestion, chronic fear and grief.

TEA THERAPY

In France, the eminent Parisian physician, Docteur Jonquet, called it "a divine herb" and, in 1685, in his treatise on coffee, tea and chocolate Philippe Sylvestre Dufour affirmed that it cured twenty-two different illnesses. In 1687, in one of the first French tea instruction manuals (*Bon usage du thé, du café et du chocolat*), the

royal physician Nicolas de Blégny had this valuable advice to offer: "I must say that tea as a tincture should be drunk piping hot, the water still boiling from the stove." For him, the addition of sugar, amber and cardamom created an especially "cordial and digestive" beverage. Many of the ideas relating to the medicinal benefits of tea were fantastical, misplaced or wildly exaggerated. To some it should be smoked with tobacco while Princess Palatine wrote on 26 February 1706 that tea rhymed with chastity: "It is an essential beverage for Protestant ministers and Catholic priests, excluded from wedlock, as it makes one chaste". By the end of the 18th century, the excitement had calmed and the nobility began to appreciate tea simply as tea.

THE LATEST IN-THING

In France, tea was not as widespread as coffee, unlike in England where, due to

the country's trade monopoly, it replaced coffee entirely. Tea was a status symbol. Still very expensive, it was drunk in the salons of Anglophile Parisians and of the elite in Bordeaux who had trade connections with the UK. Buffets loaded with pastries and petit-fours were served "English-style", i.e. guests served themselves, unaided by house-servants. The practice brought a whole new panoply of tea-related paraphernalia and tea services produced by the most prestigious craftsmen, which became fashionable among the high-society as gifts and collectibles. The Louvre Museum is home to a magnificent tea,

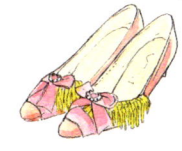

coffee and chocolate service that King Louis XV offered to his wife Marie Leszczyńska in 1729 for the birth of their son, the Dauphin.

SERVICE WITH STYLE

Tea services were first imported from China but European manufactories gradually elaborated their own formulae for porcelain. Their first models were influenced by Asian aesthetics but they soon developed their own styles. Technical innovation allowed for a broader palette of colors and the creation of motifs of exceptional finesse. Founded in 1738 by Louis XV's mistress, Madame de Pompadour, the Sèvres royal manufactory developed an international reputation. Its creations were the envy of the world and extensively copied. Silverware underwent the same revolution and the ribbing, fluting and gadroons of silver teapots from the time are astounding.

THE EMPRESS'S TEAROOM

In France in the second half of the 19th century, tea drinking became more widespread. Tearooms opened, cafés began to serve tea and tea appeared in the parlors of the rich. In keeping with the ostentation of the Second Empire, Empress Eugénie added a cachet of imperial approval by organizing tea receptions at her residence in Compiègne.

Her reception rooms were specially designed and furnished in line with the eclectic tastes of the day, combining Chinese elements, 18th century revival features and modern silk-upholstered furnishings. Every afternoon, Eugénie would welcome a dozen guests for conversation, an event that was considered a royal favor among its exclusive participants – court notables on hunting vacation in autumn.

Savory Tartlets

Makes 30 tartlets
Preparation: 30 minutes
Cooking time: 8 minutes

Beaufort tartlets

Drying time: 10 minutes

5 tbsp | 75 ml heavy (double) cream
1 organic egg
¾ cup (6 ⅓ oz) | 180 g cream cheese
3 oz | 90 g Beaufort cheese
1 pinch of ground Espelette pepper (or hot Paprika)
1 pinch of table salt

Tartlet shells
See Basic Recipes, p. 296

Equipment
Piping bag fitted with a plain tip, ½ inch | 10 mm

1. Make shells as indicated in the Basic Recipe, p. 296.

2. Prepare the Beaufort powder: preheat the oven to 325°F | 165°C | gas mark 3. Grate the Beaufort onto parchment paper and allow to dry in the oven for 10 minutes. When the cheese is perfectly dry, process in a blender to obtain a powder.

3. Prepare the savory custard filling: preheat the oven to 350°F | 180°C | gas mark 4. Whisk together the cream and egg. Add salt and Espelette pepper at the end. Generously fill the shells with the custard and place in oven for 8 minutes. If the filling falls, refill and bake again. Allow to cool.

4. Pipe cream cheese domes: with the piping bag, create a dome of cream cheese for each tartlet. Garnish with an even sprinkle of Beaufort powder.

5 tbsp | 75 ml heavy (double) cream
1 organic egg
½ cup + 2 tbsp (5 oz) | 150 g cream cheese
3 ¾ oz | 105 g sliced, smoked salmon
1 lime
1 pinch of ground Espelette pepper (or hot Paprika)
1 pinch of table salt

Tartlet shells
See Basic Recipes, p. 296

Equipment
Pastry cutters, 1 ¼ inch | 3 ½ cm diameter
Piping bag fitted with a plain tip, ½ inch | 10 mm

Salmon tartlets

1. Make shells as indicated in the Basic Recipe, p. 296.

2. Press the lime and mix the juice with the cream cheese.

3. Prepare the savory custard filling: preheat the oven to 350°F | 180°C | gas mark 4. Whisk together the cream and egg. Add salt and Espelette pepper at the end. Generously fill the shells with the custard and place in oven for 8 minutes. If the filling falls, refill and bake again. Allow to cool.

4. With the pastry cutter, cut out 30 disks of salmon the same size as the tartlets. Place a disk on top of the custard of each tartlet.

5. Pipe cream domes: with piping bag fitted with its tip, pipe a dome of cream cheese on each disk of salmon. Garnish with the lime zest and a dab of ground Espelette pepper.

Toasted seed tartlets

5 tbsp | 75 ml heavy (double) cream
1 organic egg
¾ cup (6 ⅓ oz) | 180 g cream cheese
1 heaping tsp of pumpkin seeds
1 heaping tsp of brown flax seeds
1 heaping tsp of golden flax seeds
1 heaping tsp of sunflower seeds
1 pinch of ground Espelette pepper (or hot Paprika)
1 pinch of table salt

Tartlet shells
See Basic Recipes, p. 296

Equipment
Piping bag fitted with a plain tip, ½ inch | 10 mm

1. Make shells as indicated in the Basic Recipe, p. 296.

2. Toast the seeds separately either by placing in a preheated oven at 325°F | 165°C | gas mark 3 for 6–7 minutes or in a dry frying pan.

3. Prepare the savory custard filling: preheat the oven to 350°F | 180°C | gas mark 4. Whisk together the cream and egg. Add salt and Espelette pepper at the end. Generously fill the shells with the custard and place in oven for 8 minutes. If the filling falls, refill and bake again. Allow to cool.

4. Pipe cream cheese domes: with the piping bag, create a dome of cream cheese for each tartlet. Garnish with an even sprinkle of toasted seeds.

Taramasalata tartlets

5 tbsp | 75 ml heavy (double) cream
1 organic egg
8 oz | 225 g pink taramasalata
12 g pansy blossoms
1 pinch of ground Espelette pepper (or hot Paprika)
1 pinch of table salt

Tartlet shells
See Basic Recipes, p. 296

Equipment
Piping bag fitted with a plain tip, ½ inch | 10 mm

1. Make shells as indicated in the Basic Recipe, p. 296.

2. Prepare the savory custard filling: preheat the oven to 350°F | 180°C | gas mark 4. Whisk together the cream and egg. Add salt and Espelette pepper at the end. Generously fill the shells with the custard and place in oven for 8 minutes. If the filling falls, refill and bake again. Allow to cool.

3. Pipe taramasalata domes: with the piping bag, create a dome of taramasalata on each tartlet. Garnish with pansy blossoms.

Pastrami tartlets

5 tbsp | 75 ml heavy (double) cream
1 organic egg
1 ¼ cup | 150 g *crème fraîche* (40% fat content)
1 oz + 3 oz | 30 g + 90 g pastrami
1 sheet of gelatin (¼ tbsp | 2 g powdered gelatin)
1 pinch of ground Espelette pepper (or hot Paprika)
1 pinch of table salt

Tartlet shells
See Basic Recipes, p. 296

Equipment
Fine mesh sieve
Piping bag fitted with a plain tip, ½ inch | 10 mm

1. Make shells as indicated in the Basic Recipe, p. 296.

2. Prepare the pastrami powder. Preheat the oven to 250°F | 120°C | gas mark ½. Place 1 oz | 30 g of pastrami on a baking sheet lined in parchment paper and dry in the oven for 1 hour. When it is dry and crispy, process it in a blender to obtain a fine powder.

3. Make the pastrami cream: chop the remaining pastrami. Heat the heavy cream and add the pastrami, leaving it to infuse for 20 minutes. Soften the gelatin in cold water. Strain the cream through the sieve. Squeeze all the water out of the gelatin and place in warm cream to melt. Blend and season to taste.
Place the pastrami cream in the piping bag fitted with the tip. Allow to firm up in the refrigerator for a minimum of 30 minutes.

4. Prepare the savory custard filling: preheat the oven to 350°F | 180°C | gas mark 4. Whisk together the *créme fraîche* and egg. Add salt and Espelette pepper at the end. Generously fill the shells with the custard and place in oven for 8 minutes. If the filling falls, refill and bake again. Allow to cool.

5. Pipe pastrami cream domes with piping bag. Garnish with an even sprinkle of pastrami powder.

Chive tartlets

5 tbsp | 75 ml heavy (double) cream
1 organic egg
¾ cup (6 ⅓ oz) | 180 g cream cheese
⅓ oz | 9 g chives
1 pinch of ground Espelette pepper (or hot Paprika)
1 pinch of table salt

Tartlet shells
See Basic Recipes, p. 296

Equipment
Piping bag fitted with a plain tip, ½ inch | 10 mm

1. Make shells as indicated in the Basic Recipe, p. 296.

2. Wash and mince the chives.

3. Prepare the savory custard filling: preheat the oven to 350°F | 180°C | gas mark 4. Whisk together the cream and egg. Add salt and Espelette pepper at the end. Generously fill the shells with the custard and place in oven for 8 minutes. If the filling falls, refill and bake again. Allow to cool.

4. Pipe cream domes: with the piping bag, create a dome of cream cheese for each tartlet. Garnish with an even sprinkle of minced chives.

Pairs well with
Our *Darjeeling* or *Ceylan* tea

Cocktail Bites

Makes 30 bites of each variety
Preparation: 25–35 minutes
Cooking time: 10 minutes

Preparation time for the rillettes:
15 minutes

1 large cucumber
1 oz | 30 g salmon roe
1 punnet of red-veined sorrel microgreens
Ground Espelette pepper
Table salt

Salmon rillettes

3 ¾ oz | 100 g raw salmon, Red Label (or any certified sea-raised salmon)
2 oz | 50 g sliced smoked salmon
4 tsp | 20 g cream cheese
5 sprigs of chives
Juice of ½ a lemon
1 cup | 300 ml heavy (double) cream
1 drop of organic olive oil
1 pinch of Espelette pepper (or hot Paprika)
1 pinch of *fleur de sel* (or other coarse sea salt)

Equipment
Small melon baller

Cucumber with salmon rillettes

1. Prepare the salmon rillettes as indicated in the recipe for Mimosa Eggs, p. 58.

2. Cut the cucumber into ⅔ inch | 2 cm logs. Scoop out ½ of the flesh with the melon baller.

3. Quickly blanch the cucumber logs in salted, boiling water and plunge them in a large bowl of water and ice. Drain.

4. With a small spoon, fill the logs to slightly overflowing with the rillettes.

5. Garnish with the microgreens, a pinch of Espelette pepper and the salmon roe.

• • •

Carrots with Zaatar goat cheese

8 large carrots with their greens intact
7 oz | 200 g young goat cheese
4 pinches of Lebanese Zaatar spice mix
2 ¼ tbsp | 40 ml Corsican olive oil
Ground Espelette pepper (or hot Paprika)
Fleur de sel (or other coarse sea salt)
Table salt

Equipment

Pastry cutter 1 inch | 3 cm in diameter
Small melon baller
Piping bag fitted with a plain tip, ⅓ inch | 8 mm

1. Peel and wash the carrots, saving the greens for the garnish. Cut the carrots into ⅔ inch | 2 cm logs. Stand the logs on end and with the pastry cutter, cut 1 inch | 3 cm diameter cylinders. With the melon baller, scoop out a well in the middle.

2. Place the carrots in boiling, salted water and cook through. Refresh them in a bowl of ice and water. Drain.

3. Mix the goat cheese with the spices, olive oil, a pinch of *fleur de sel* and a pinch of Espelette pepper. Place the cheese mixture in the piping bag and pipe domes of goat cheese in the carrot cylinders. Garnish with a dab of Espelette pepper and a sprig of carrot greens.

Chef's tip

If the goat cheese is too wet, drain in a clean cloth all night before starting.

Stuffed creminis

1 lb 3 oz | 540 g white button mushrooms
30 medium size cremini mushrooms
6 sprigs of flat leaf parsley
2 tbsp | 30 g salted butter
½ cup | 200 ml heavy (double) cream
Ground Espelette pepper (or hot Paprika)
Fleur de sel (or other coarse sea salt)
Table salt

1. Make a mushroom duxelles: clean the button mushrooms then dice them. In a saucepan, melt the butter and sweat the diced mushrooms. When they are cooked, deglaze with the cream. Reduce the mixture and stir in the minced parsley. Season with salt and Espelette pepper.

2. Prepare the creminis: clean the mushrooms and remove the stems. Blanch the tops in salted boiling water then refresh them in iced water. They should be cooked but still firm to hold their shape.

3. Mound the duxelles in each cap. Season with the *fleur de sel* and Espelette pepper. Garnish with a leaf of parsley.

Chef's tip

Choose very firm creminis. Make sure the cut stems are not darkened or dry. Also check that the caps are firm and evenly colored.

Potatoes and caviar

10 large Agria potatoes
1 oz | 30 g French caviar
½ cup + 5 tbsp | 100 g *crème fraîche*
(40 % fat content)
15 sprigs of chives
2 tsp | 10 g superfine capers
10 slices of white bread
1 ½ tbsp | 30 g clarified butter,
see recipe p. 88
30 small borage flowers

Equipment
Pastry cutter, 1 inch | 3 cm and
½ inch | 1 ½ cm diameter
Small melon baller
Piping bag with a plain tip of
½ inch | 8 mm diameter

1. Peel and wash the potatoes. Cut them in pieces ²/₃ inch | 2 cm long. Stand them on a cut side and with the 1 inch | 3 cm pastry cutter, cut out cylinders. Scoop out the inside with a melon baller.

2. Steam the cylinders until they are cooked through. Check with the tip of a sharp blade*.

3. Mince the chives and the capers. Add both to the *crème fraîche* before putting the mixture into the piping bag.

4. Preheat the oven to 350°F | 170°C | gas mark 4. With a pastry brush, brush clarified butter on both sides of each slice of sandwich bread. Cut small disks out of the sandwich bread with the cutter (½ inch | 1 ½ cm). Bake at 350°F | 170°C | gas mark 4, between two baking sheets for 10–15 minutes.

5. Shape a dome of cream onto each potato cylinder. Garnish with a crouton, a point of caviar and a borage blossom.

Chef's tip

To check the potatoes, slip the tip of a thin blade into the middle. It should enter and pull out easily. Pay careful attention when cooking the potatoes.

Refrigeration time: 20 minutes

5 daikon radishes
5 ⅓ oz | 150 g Mediterranean red tuna loin
⅓ cup | 75 ml organic Corsican olive
10 sprigs of coriander
10 pansies
Ground Espelette pepper (or hot Paprika)
Fleur de sel (or other coarse sea salt)
Table salt

Horseradish cream
2 cups | 250 g *crème fraîche* (40 % fat content)
½ tsp | 1 g grated horseradish
1 sheet of gelatin (¼ tbsp | 2 g powdered gelatin)
1 pinch of *fleur de sel* (or other coarse sea salt)

Equipment
Pastry cutter 1 inch | 3 cm diameter
Small melon baller

Pairs well with
Our *Yunnan* tea

•••

Radishes and red tuna

1. Prepare the horseradish cream: soften the gelatin in cold water. Mix the *crème fraîche* and the horseradish. Heat until it is quite warm. Wring out the gelatin and add to the cream. Stir the mixture until the gelatin has melted. Add the *fleur de sel* and adjust the seasoning.

2. Pour the hot cream onto a baking sheet and allow it to firm up in the refrigerator for 20 minutes. Once chilled, dice into cubes of ¹⁄₁₀ inch | 3 mm.

3. Peel the daikon radishes and cut ⅔ inch | 2 cm logs. Place the logs on a cut side and with the pastry cutter, cut out cylinders with a 1 inch | 3 cm diameter. Scoop out the middle with a melon baller.

4. Blanch the cylinders for 5 seconds in salted, boiling water. Refresh them in iced water.

5. Dice the tuna finely (as for a tartare). Season the tuna with olive oil, *fleur de sel*, Espelette pepper, the cubes of horseradish cream and the minced coriander.

6. Fill the radish cylinders with the tuna mixture, allowing it to overflow slightly. Season and garnish with a pansy petal.

Bordeaux Cannelés

Makes 20 cannelés
Preparation: 30 minutes
Cooking time: 1 hour
Resting time: 24 hours
Infusion time: 1 hour

1 vanilla pod
2 cups + 2 tbsp | 500 ml whole milk
3 ½ tbsp | 50 g butter +
3 tbsp | 40 g for molds
2 organic eggs + 2 organic egg yolks
2 cups | 240 g confectioners' (icing) sugar
1 ½ tbsp dark aged rum (rhum agricole if possible)
1 cup | 130 g cake (SR) flour
- 2 tbsp | 20 g for molds

Equipment
20 cannelés molds, 2 inch | 5 ½ cm diameter

Prepare the cannelé batter the day before.

1. With a sharp knife, slice the vanilla pod half lengthwise. Using the tip, scrape the interior to remove the seeds. Pour the milk into a saucepan, add the vanilla pod and seeds and bring to a boil. Remove from heat, cover and allow to infuse for 1 hour. Remove vanilla pod and allow to cool.
Melt butter and allow to cool. Sift the confectioners' sugar and flour into separate bowls. In a large bowl, whisk together the eggs, egg yolks and confectioners' sugar. Continue to beat and add the following ingredients one after another, in this order: rum, melted butter, sifted flour and the vanilla-infused milk.
Refrigerate batter for at least 12 hours.

2. Butter the cannelé molds with softened butter and refrigerate for 15 minutes to allow the butter to harden. Dust with flour, turn upside down and tap out any excess. Keep in refrigerator until ready to fill with batter.

Pairs well with
Our *Marie-Antoinette* tea

...

They must be filled just before being placed in a hot oven.

3. Preheat the oven to 350°F | 180° C | gas mark 4. Fill the chilled molds to ⅕ inch | ½ cm below the rim. Place in oven and bake for 1 hour. If the cannelés puff up during this time, prick the top with the tip of a knife. The cannelés should be dark brown on the outside. The French expression states, "When it's black, it's done". Immediately remove from molds and place onto a rack to cool.
Serve at room temperature.

Chef's tip

The cannelés do not keep. You must eat them the same day. However, you can prepare the batter and keep it in the refrigerator for 2 to 3 days. Mix the batter before each use.
The type of mold is important. If possible, avoid using silicone and opt for copper for incomparable results.

TEA ETIQUETTE

The 19th century French lifestyle "guru", Baroness Staffe was a stickler for etiquette. Naturally she had her own very rigorous requirements for the tea ritual :

TIMING

"Green tea (yellow leaf) is the Chinese Château Lafite and is only imbibed in aristocratic households. […] Gateaux should not be dunked into the tea accompanying them especially if they make crumbs. Tea is not soup.
"With tea as for coffee, when one's cup is empty, the spoon should be placed on the saucer, not in the cup. This precaution prevents accidents."
To Baroness Staffe, one should never blow tea to cool it and the addition of cold water is a total no-no. The cup should be raised with the saucer. When invited to tea one should be on time and not stay overstay one's welcome.

THE PERFECT MISTRESS OF CEREMONY

Tea is first prepared and then served in the drawing room. Each cup should be on its own saucer, never piled and accompanied by the sugar bowl, sugar tongs, teaspoons, a small pot of cold milk and a small dish containing rounds of lemon. Before serving, the mistress of the house should inquire how guests like their tea, then present the teacup on its saucer with the left hand while serving from the teapot with the right. Sugar is always offered before lemon as a chemical reaction prevents sugar from dissolving in lemon-infused tea. The lemon should not be pressed with a spoon to extract the juice. Once all guests have been served, pastries may be passed around, in individual portions or cut into slices. Each guest should have their own dessert plate, a cake fork and a small cocktail napkin.

Fraisier

Serves 8 people
Preparation: 2 ½ hours
Cooking time: 30 minutes
Resting time: 2 hours

Almond génoise cake
3 ½ tbsp | 50 g butter +
1 ½ tbsp | 20 g for the mold
1 ⅔ cups | 200 g cake (SR) flour +
2 ½ tbsp for the mold
6 organic eggs
1 cup | 200 g granulated sugar
½ cup | 50 g ground almonds
(almond flour)

Vanilla syrup
½ cup – 1 tbsp | 100 ml water
½ cup | 100 g granulated sugar
½ vanilla pod

Vanilla mousseline cream
6 ½ tbsp | 90 g butter
¾ cup | 180 ml whole milk
2 organic egg yolks
¼ cup | 50 g granulated sugar

ALMOND GÉNOISE AND VANILLA SYRUP

1. Melt the 1 ½ tbsp of butter. Using a pastry brush, butter the cake pan. Refrigerate for 15 minutes for the butter to harden.
Sift the flour. In a small saucepan, melt the 3 ½ tbsp | 50 g of butter over low heat.

2. In a large heatproof mixing bowl, whisk together the eggs and sugar.
Preheat the oven to 325°F | 165°F | gas mark 3.
Place the mixing bowl over a pan of gently simmering water and whisk until the mixture is warm (approximately 122°F | 50°C), thick and pale, and has tripled in volume. This should take 10 minutes with an electric mixer and 15 minutes with a whisk. Remove from heat and continue to beat until the mixture has completely cooled down.

2 tbsp | 15 g cornstarch (cornflour)
1 vanilla pod
4 ⅔ cups | 700 g strawberries

Pink almond paste
1 cup | 250 g almond paste
Red food coloring

Equipment
Round cake pan with straight sides (8 ½ to 9 inch | 21 to 22 cm diameter
Round ring mold, 8 inch | 20 cm diameter
Piping bag fitted with a ½ inch | 10 mm plain tip
Candy (sugar) thermometer

3. Using a rubber spatula, fold in the sifted flour little by little, then the ground almonds and finally, the melted butter. To gently mix together, start with the spatula in the center of the bowl, work up the sides of the bowl and bring back down towards the center, all the while turning the bowl regularly.
This will result in a smooth and homogenous mixture. Lightly flour the cake pan and turn upside down to tap out any excess. Immediately fill with batter, place in oven and bake for approximately 30 minutes.

4. While the génoise is baking, prepare the vanilla syrup.
In a saucepan, bring ½ cup – 1 tbsp | 100 ml water and sugar to a boil. Add the vanilla seeds from the scraped pod. Allow to cool.
Check to see if the génoise is done by inserting the tip of a knife into the center. When the cake is ready, the knife should come out clean, dry and free of crumbs.
Remove from oven. Allow to cool for 5 minutes before removing from the mold and placing on a rack. Allow to cool completely.

VANILLA MOUSSELINE CREAM
5. Remove butter from the refrigerator to soften.
In a saucepan, bring the milk and the seeds grated from the vanilla pod to a simmer.

6. In a large bowl, whisk the egg yolks and sugar until slightly pale. Incorporate the cornstarch. Pour ⅓ of the hot milk over the mixture of egg yolks, sugar and cornstarch. Whisk together and pour the whole mixture back into the saucepan. Bring to a boil while stirring with a whisk, making sure to scrape down the sides of the pan with a spatula.

7. Remove from heat and allow to cool for 10 minutes so that it is hot but not boiling. Incorporate half of the butter. Allow the cream to cool to room temperature (64°F to 68°F | 18°C to 20°C). If it is still hot, refrigerate for 10 minutes to finish cooling off. Meanwhile, wash the strawberries, drain on a dish towel and hull.
In a large bowl, whip the cooled mousseline cream with an electric mixer until smooth. Add the remaining half of the butter.
Whip until the cream is emulsified and smooth.

ASSEMBLY

8. Using a serrated knife, remove the thin, dark crust from the génoise, then slice horizontally to create a disk of cake, ⅖ inch | 1 cm thick. Cut the disk to fit properly in the pastry ring (you can place the ring on top of the cake and push down).

9. Place the cake ring on a cake stand or cake platter and fit the first disk of génoise inside. Lightly soak with vanilla syrup.

Pairs well with
Our *Joséphine* tea

Transfer the mousseline cream to the piping bag fitted with a plain tip. Pipe a layer of cream in a spiral on top of the cake. Arrange a border of strawberries (sliced in half) around the inside of the mold. Place the berries so that the cut side will be visible when unmolding the cake.
Fill the center with whole strawberries, pushing down on the cream so that it rises between the strawberries. Cover with mousseline cream, filling the gaps and creating a flat surface. Fill with the remaining mousseline cream to the very edge of the mold and smooth the surface.

ALMOND PASTE FOR TOP OF CAKE
10. Using your hands, mix the almond paste and red food coloring. On a clean work surface, roll out this mixture extremely thin (1 mm). Cover the cake with this sheet and trim the excess.
Place the Fraisier in the refrigerator for 2 hours. Carefully remove the ring and decorate the cake with the remaining strawberries, sliced in half.

Chef's tip

To prepare a Framboisier, replace the 4 ⅔ cups | 700 g of strawberries with 5 ⅔ cups | 700 g of raspberries.

THE BENEFITS OF TEA

When tea first appeared in France in the 17th century, it was hailed for its medicinal and curative properties.

"CURTAIL VAPORS OF THE BRAIN"

In medical and household treatises, the claims of tea's healing powers were legion. In his *La Maison réglée, et l'art de diriger la maison d'un grand seigneur* [An Ordered House and the Art of Managing the Mansion of a Nobleman] (1692) François Audiger notes that tea is drunk in the morning "to wake the mind and stir the appetite", while after a meal it is drunk "to aid digestion". Above all, it "curtails vapors of the brain and refreshes and purifies the blood". Were Audiger's ideas entirely fanciful? Interestingly, recent scientific research has pointed to tea's positive effects on stress (or "vapors of the brain") and on the prevention of cardiovascular diseases.

KEEP CALM AND DRINK TEA

Among the various beneficial effects of green tea, the antioxidant effect of its polyphenols has attracted a great deal of attention. Antioxidants protect our cells against the free radicals responsible for aging. The cosmetics industry uses tea polyphenols in anti-wrinkle cream. Research has also studied how they reduce bad cholesterol and hardening of the arteries.

Also contained in tea is: fluoride – 0.3 mg per cup; gold – 1 mg per day helps preserve tooth enamel. Theine meanwhile stimulates the central nervous system, boosting mental awareness and physical activity. Other research meanwhile has investigated the feel-good, calming virtues of tea.

Chocolate and Coffee Macarons

Makes approximately 50 macarons
Preparation: 2 hours
Cooking time: 12–15 minutes
Resting time: minimum of 13 hours

Macaron shells
See Basic Recipes, p. 300
1 level tbsp | 17 g unsweetened cocoa powder

Chocolate ganache
10 oz | 290 g chocolate, minimum 70% cocoa
1 cup + 2 tbsp | 270 ml heavy (double) cream
4 tbsp | 60 g butter

Equipment
A piping bag fitted with a plain tip, ½ inch | 10 mm

CHOCOLATE GANACHE

1. Prepare the ganache. Cut the butter in small pieces and set aside. With a sharp knife, chop the chocolate into small pieces. Place in a large bowl. In a saucepan, bring the cream to a boil and pour a third of the chocolate in at a time. Stir with a wooden spatula between each addition to obtain a creamy mass.
Stir in the butter until you have a smooth, glossy cream. Transfer the ganache into a baking dish and cover with plastic wrap, making sure it directly touches the entire surface of the ganache.
Allow the ganache to cool to room temperature. Place in the refrigerator for 1 hour until it has the consistency of creamed butter.

MACARON SHELLS

2. Follow the basic macaron recipe on p. 300. Make sure to sift the cocoa powder with the almond flour and confectioners' sugar.

•••

ASSEMBLY

3. When the ganache has the consistency of creamed butter, place it in the piping bag fitted with its tip. Pipe a walnut-sized amount of ganache on half of the macaron shells. Top each with the remaining shells.
Keep macarons in an airtight container in the refrigerator for 12 hours before serving.

Variation: coffee macarons

1. For this variation, prepare the macaron batter and simply replace the powdered cocoa with the instant coffee powder.

2. Prepare the coffee cream: Preheat the oven to 285°F | 145°C | gas mark 1 ½. Spread the coffee beans on a baking sheet and roast for 15 minutes. Crush the beans.
Bring the cream to a boil. Add the coffee beans and stir. Allow to infuse overnight (8 hours).
Filter the cream (carefully pressing down on all the solids to extract all the coffee aromas) and stir in the cornstarch. Pour the mixture into a saucepan.
Add sugar and stir well until it dissolves. Bring to a boil. Remove from heat and add the chopped white chocolate. Blend well with a stick blender. Allow to rest for 2 minutes before adding the butter. Blend again to obtain a smooth, creamy mass. Place inside the piping bag and assemble as above.

Macaron shells
See Basic Recipes, p. 300
1 level tbsp | 10 g instant coffee powder

Coffee cream
1 ¼ cup | 290 ml heavy (double) cream
1 ¾ oz | 50 g coffee beans
2 tbsp | 20 g cornstarch (cornflour)
½ cup | 100 g granulated sugar
5 oz | 140 g white chocolate (chopped)
7 tbsp | 100 g butter (diced)

Pairs well with
Our *Eugénie* tea

Savarins

Makes 8 savarins
Preparation: 2 ½ hours
Cooking time: 25 minutes
Resting time: 1 hour

Baba dough
½ oz | 12 g fresh yeast
2 tbsp | 20 ml water
2 cups | 250 g cake (SR) flour
1 pinch of *fleur de sel* (or other coarse sea salt)
1 ¼ tbsp | 15 g granulated sugar
4 organic eggs
5 tbsp | 75 g butter +
1 ½ tbsp | 20 g for molds

Rum syrup
4 ¼ cups | 1 litre water
1 ¼ cups | 250 g granulated sugar
1 lemon, unwaxed
1 orange, unwaxed
1 vanilla pod
½ cup | 120 ml aged rum
+ ½ cup | 125 ml aged rum for final glaze

BABA DOUGH

1. Cut the butter into small pieces and allow to soften at room temperature. Crumble the yeast with your fingers and dilute with 2 tbsp room temperature water. In a large bowl, place the flour, salt and sugar. Add the diluted yeast and 2 eggs. Start mixing with a wooden spatula until the dough pulls away from the sides of the bowl. Add 1 egg. Knead until the dough pulls away from the sides of the bowl again. Repeat this process with the last egg.
Incorporate the softened butter into the dough and continue to knead until the dough once again pulls away from the sides of the bowl.

2. Cover the dough with a damp tea towel or plastic wrap. Allow to double in volume at room temperature (approximately 1 hour).

3. Preheat the oven to 325° F | 165 °C | gas mark 3. Butter the molds.

Garnish

2 ¾ cups | 325 ml sweetened whipped heavy (double) cream
Seasonal fruits for decoration

Equipment

8 savarin molds (2 ¾ inch | 7 cm diameter rings)
Piping bag without tip
Piping bag fitted with a ½ inch | 10 mm star tip

Pairs well with

Our *Roi Soleil* tea

Chef's tip

If you have a stand mixer, prepare the dough in the bowl of the mixer fitted with the dough hook attachment.
You can also mix the ingredients in a food processor.

Transfer dough to piping bag without tip and fill molds. Allow dough to double in volume and rise up to the edges of the molds. Place in oven and bake for 20 minutes.

RUM SYRUP

4. Pour water and sugar into a saucepan. Using a vegetable peeler, remove the orange and lemon zests (avoiding the bitter white pith). Juice both fruits. With a sharp knife, slice the vanilla pod in half lengthwise. Using the tip, scrape the interior to remove the seeds.

In the saucepan, bring to a boil the water and sugar with vanilla pod and seeds, the juice and zests of both the orange and lemon. Remove from heat, strain through a fine mesh sieve and add the rum.

5. Transfer the syrup to a baking dish that is large enough to hold the baked savarins. Turn pastries around in the syrup, dipping bottoms and tops, until well soaked.

Place a wire rack on a large dish or rimmed baking sheet, and place savarins on the rack. Reheat the remaining syrup. When hot, drizzle over the cakes several times. Allow to cool.

ASSEMBLY

6. Place the savarins on a serving platter and drizzle generously with rum.

Using the piping bag fitted with the star tip, top each cake with sweetened whipped cream. Decorate with seasonal fruits.

THE PERFECT TEAPOT

Any self-respecting tea-aholic should own not one but several teapots – ideally one for each family of tea.

MEMORIES OF TEA

Tea impregnates teapots with its aromas, so by keeping teapots separate, you can preserve flavors. Porcelain teapots are *de rigueur* for green tea, Darjeeling, Oolong and fragranced teas. Cast-iron teapots are ideal for smoked and black teas. Clay teapots are perfect for Ceylon and broken-leaf teas; metal teapots should only be used for mint tea. In the tea world there are two types of people: those who prefer a virgin pot and those who like their teapots caked with residue so that all the tannins and aromas of brews-gone-by linger on to enhance future brewing. Whatever the approach, never wash your teapot with detergent or in the dishwasher.

BEST POT PRACTICE

Before adding the tea, warm the teapot with boiling water. The English stir the pot with a spoon or, as George Orwell advises in his essay "A Nice Cup of Tea", one should "give the pot a good shake" before allowing the leaves to settle. A smaller teapot helps aromas express themselves better – it's a good idea to create several brews in the same small teapot than in one large teapot as the aromas get lost. A teapot is preferable over a tea ball strainer as a teapot allows the leaves to swell and relax. It is also possible to steep loose tea-leaves in one teapot then strain the tea into a tea service.

TEA in the Garden

Tea in the Garden

The undulating rows of tea plants descending a valley in green waves provide a vision of nature at its most divine that somehow makes its way into the cup. Drinking tea is about getting back to nature and letting the mind wander.

HARMONY WITH NATURE

There's nothing more delectable than taking tea in the garden in the shade of a tree. The flavors and aromas of tea seem to blend with the fragrances of nature. Tea's dominant notes are all plant-based: whether grass, herbs, and straw; floral fragrances such as rose, orange blossom, and violet; or succulent scents such as fruits, berries and vanilla. Tea has a vast aromatic palette that is a sheer pleasure to explore.

To Chinese and Japanese tea-masters, tea has a special relationship to nature conveying a sacred message: the moment when tea touches the palate is an instant of harmony between the self and the universe. Focusing so completely on the present provides a haven of peace as the crazy world turns and churns around us. This partly explains its remarkable calming effect.

FLORAL TEA

Tea is an ode to nature, a magical moment expressed in the Chinese tradition of "flowering tea". Dried leaves are bound around dried flowers into a bulb so that, when steeped, the bundle unfurls and blooms, as if by magic, to reveal the flower inside. A wonder to behold. Above all, tea has a magnificent ability to capture and then release fragrances. This was something the Chinese realized centuries ago during the Song period (960–1279), when they developed a simple technique to produce aromatic tea by layering dried tea and dried flowers, which infused the leaves with floral fragrances.

Jasmine tea is the most famous example, but chrysanthemum, magnolia, rose and lotus are also widespread. The West further developed the tradition, making aromatic black teas with fruit essences, notably with bergamot to

produce Earl Grey.

Since the 1980s, aromatic teas have become more sophisticated, as food fragrances and manufacturing techniques have come on in leaps and bounds during this period.

TEA GARDENS

The British are passionate gardeners and consummate tea drinkers, so it's no surprise that the garden has become the privileged home to tea drinking. In the 18th century, the Vauxhall and Ranelagh pleasure gardens in London were especially designed to savor tea in attractive, natural surroundings, and help turn tea drinking into a high-society experience.

Each year, the Queen welcomes over 30,000 guests to her famous Buckingham Palace garden parties. At each party, 27,000 cups of tea, 20,000 sandwiches and 20,000 slices of cake are consumed. The events are an important way for the Queen to speak to a broad range of people from all walks of life.

CHANIWA

The Japanese firmly believe in the relationship between tea and nature. Landscape design, art and the sacred encounter with tea come together in *chaniwa*, tea gardens dedicated to the art of tea drinking.

A tea garden provides a meditative stroll amid the elements. Visitors meander through a meticulously landscaped garden, releasing the weight of daily life as they approach the sacred heart of the garden, the *chashitsu*, or teahouse. Cut off from the outside world, time is suspended. Nothing in a tea garden is left to chance. Each plant is chosen according to aesthetic principles, with a preference for moss, ferns and evergreens. There are few bright flowers so as not to disturb contemplation. Asymmetry is central and Japanese gardens are not laid on straight axes, but meander through the meticulously trimmed vegetation, encountering traditional features such as stone lanterns and water basins, garden bridges and ablutions basins. At the end of the path, the soul is purified and the visitor is ready to settle in the tea pavilion for the tea ceremony. A journey through Zen that ends in a tea cup!

Savory Cakes

Makes 30 mini cakes of each variety
Preparation: 40 minutes
Cooking time: 13 minutes

Summer garden cakes

Drying time (powder): 3 hours

1 ½ cups | 400 ml of whole milk
4 oz | 115 g all-purpose flour
2 ½ tsp | 8 g baker's yeast
⅓ cup | 75 g unsalted butter, creamed
2 organic eggs
1 ⅔ oz | 45 g yellow zucchini
1 ⅔ oz | 45 g green zucchini
⅔ oz | 20 g spinach
Olive oil
2 pinches of ground Espelette pepper (or hot Paprika)
2 pinches of table salt

Green pea powder (¾ cup | 100 g)
⅔ cup | 100 g frozen peas

Garnish (see recipe)
¼ cup | 50 g cream cheese
¾ cup | 100 g green pea powder

1. Start with the spinach purée: Drop ⅔ oz | 20 g of spinach in a saucepan of salted boiling water. Cook for 3 minutes. Drain and blend with ⅘ cup | 200 ml of ice water to obtain a perfectly smooth purée. Set aside.

2. Prepare the green pea powder: preheat the oven to 150°F | 70°C | gas mark ¼. Spread the frozen peas onto a baking sheet and dry in the oven for 3 hours. Blend them to obtain a bright green powder. Set aside in a dry area.

3. Dice the green and yellow zucchini finely. Quickly sauté them in the olive oil and season with a pinch of salt and a pinch of Espelette pepper. Set aside.

4. Prepare the cake batter: warm the milk in the microwave to 95°F | 35°C and stir in the yeast until dissolved. In a hemispherical bowl, whisk the eggs. Add flour, milk-leavening mixture and the creamed butter. Season with salt and pepper. Add the yellow and green zucchini and the spinach to the batter.

Equipment
2 x 24 Flexipan oval savarin molds,
1 ¾ inch | 4 cm
Piping bag fitted with a plain tip,
⅓ inch | 10 mm

Drying time (powder): 1 hour
Refrigeration: 30 minutes

1 ½ cups | 400 ml of whole milk
4 oz | 115 g all-purpose flour
2 ½ tsp | 8 g baker's yeast
⅓ cup | 75 g unsalted butter, creamed
2 organic eggs
1⅔ oz | 45 g Beaufort cheese
1 ⅔ oz | 45 g pastrami
1 pinch of ground Espelette pepper (or hot Paprika)
1 pinch of table salt

Pastrami powder
3 slices of smoked pastrami

Garnish
½ cup | 60 g *crème fraîche* (40 % fat content)

5. Preheat the oven to 350°F | 180°C | gas mark 4. Spoon the batter into the molds and place in oven for 13 minutes.

6. Prepare the garnish: put the cream cheese in the piping bag and place a dot of cream in the indent of each cooled cake. Dust with green pea powder.

Pastrami cakes

1. Start by preparing the pastrami powder. Preheat the oven to 250°F | 120°C | gas mark ½. Place the slices of smoked pastrami on a baking sheet lined with parchment paper. Allow to dry in the oven for 1 hour. When the pastrami is dry and crispy, process to obtain a fine powder.

2. Slice the Beaufort cheese and make a *brunoise* (a fine dice). Do the same for the 45 g of pastrami.

3. Prepare the cake batter: warm the milk in the microwave to 95°F | 35°C and stir in the yeast until dissolved. In a hemispherical bowl, whisk the eggs. Add flour, milk-leavening mixture and the creamed butter. Season with salt and pepper. Add the Beaufort and pastrami *brunoise* to the batter.

4. Preheat the oven to 350°F | 180°C | gas mark 4. Spoon the batter into the molds and place in oven for 13 minutes.

3 slices of pastrami
1 sheet of gelatin (¼ tbsp | 2 g powdered gelatin)

Equipment
2 x 24 Flexipan oval savarin molds, 1 ¾ inch | 4 cm
Piping bag fitted with a plain tip, ⅓ inch | 10 mm
Fine mesh sieve

Cooking time for tomatoes: 4 hours

1 ½ cups | 400 ml of whole milk
4 oz | 115 g all-purpose flour
2 ½ tsp | 8 g baker's yeast
⅓ cup | 75 g unsalted butter, creamed
2 organic eggs
⅓ cup | 55 g puréed semi-dried tomato (see recipe)
3 tbsp | 27 g black olives (pitted)
2 pinches of ground Espelette pepper (or hot Paprika)
2 pinches of table salt

5. Prepare the garnish: warm the *crème fraîche*. Chop the slices of pastrami. Place them in the warm *crème fraîche* to steep. Soften the gelatin in cold water. Strain the *crème fraîche* with the fine mesh sieve. Squeeze excess water out of the gelatin and place it in the infused *crème fraîche* until it melts. Blend and season with a pinch of Espelette pepper. Place the *crème fraîche* in a piping bag fitted with the plain tip and place in the refrigerator for 30 minutes until firm.

6. Place a dot of the *crème fraîche* in the indent of each cooled cake and dust with pastrami powder.

Tomato, Olive, Mozzarella cakes

1. Prepare the semi-dried tomatoes: preheat the oven to 195°F | 90°C | gas mark ¼. Peel the tomatoes and cut them into quarters lengthwise. Remove the seeds. Put the tomato quarters into a large bowl. Add olive oil and salt. Mix gently. Add sugar if needed. Line a baking sheet with parchment paper. Spread the tomatoes evenly across the pan, making sure there is plenty of space between them. Sprinkle with thyme and place in oven for 4 hours. Keep an eye on the tomatoes. Brush them with oil when needed. Turn over the quarters that are either too dry on top or those that are too wet on underneath. As each quarter is ready, take them out of the oven. When all the tomatoes have baked long enough, allow them to cool down.

Purée of semi-dried tomato (55 g)
1 ½ tomatoes
1 ml olive oil
1 g granulated sugar (optional)
1 sprig of thyme
1 pinch of table salt

Garnish
6 ½ tbsp | 51 g *crème fraîche* (40 % fat content)
½ oz | 12 g mozzarella di buffala DOP
1 sheet of gelatin (¼ tbsp | 2 g powdered gelatin)
1 punnet of basil microgreens
1 g ground Espelette pepper (or hot Paprika)

Equipment
2 x 24 Flexipan oval savarin molds, 1 ¾ inch | 4 cm
Piping bag fitted with a plain tip, ½ inch | 10 mm
Fine mesh sieve

Pairs well with
Our *Jasmin* tea

2. Process the tomatoes to obtain a very smooth purée. Set aside. Cut the olives into small cubes.

3. Prepare the cake batter: warm the milk in the microwave to 95°F | 35°C and add the yeast/baking powder. In a hemispherical bowl, whisk the eggs. Add flour, milk-yeast mixture and the creamed butter. Season with a pinch of salt and a pinch of Espelette pepper. Add the olives and the tomato purée to the batter. Season again with a pinch of salt and Espelette pepper.

4. Preheat the oven to 350°F | 180°C | gas mark 4. Spoon the batter into the molds and place in oven for 13 minutes.

5. Prepare the garnish: warm the *crème fraîche*. Chop the mozzarella and place it in the warm *crème fraîche* for 10 to 15 minutes to steep. Soften the gelatin in cold water. Strain the *crème fraîche* with the fine mesh sieve. Squeeze excess water out of the gelatin and place it in the infused *crème fraîche* until it melts. Blend and season. Place the *crème fraîche* in a piping bag fitted with the plain tip and place in the refrigerator for 30 minutes until firm.

6. Place a dot of the *crème fraîche* in the indent of each cooled cake and top with a basil leaf.

Rose-flavored Loaf Cake

Serves 8–10 people
Preparation: 1 ½ hours
Cooking time: 55 minutes
Resting time: 12 hours

Batter
2 ½ tbsp | 35 g butter +
1 ½ tbsp | 20 g for the mold
½ cup + 5 tbsp | 105 g flour +
2 ½ tbsp | 20 g for the mold
1 ½ tsp | ½ packet | 5 ½ g baking powder
10 ½ tbsp | 125 g granulated sugar
2 organic eggs
3 ¾ tbsp | 55 ml heavy cream
1 pinch of salt
4 tsp | 15 ml rose syrup

Rose syrup
1 ⅓ cup | 250 g granulated sugar
4 tsp | 20 ml rose water
4 tsp | 20 ml rose syrup

Equipment
Loaf pan, 10 x 3 x 3 inch | 25 x 8 x 8 cm

BATTER

1. Butter the mold. Place a strip of parchment paper at the bottom to help when unmolding. Refrigerate the mold for 10 minutes for the butter to harden. Take the mold out of the refrigerator and immediately flour it, turning it over to tap out the excess flour.

2. In a small saucepan, warm the butter until it melts. Sift the flour and baking powder into a small bowl. Pour the sugar into a medium-sized bowl and add the eggs one at a time, whipping well after each addition. Add the cream, a pinch of salt and the rose syrup while you continue to whip.
With a rubber spatula, fold the flour-baking powder into the mixture. Finally, fold in the melted butter.

3. Preheat oven to 410°F | 210°C | gas mark 6. Pour the batter into the mold. Place in oven and bake for 10 minutes. Remove from oven and with a sharp knife, slice the crust lengthwise.

•••

Place back in oven and bake at 350°F | 180°C | gas mark 4 and bake for 45 minutes.
The cake is done when a sharp knife inserted in the middle comes out clean, dry and free of crumbs.

ROSE SYRUP
4. While the cake is baking, prepare the syrup.
Bring 1 cup + 4 ¼ tbsp | 300 ml water, sugar, rose water and rose syrup to a boil. Remove from heat.

GARNISH
5. When the cake is done, unmold onto a cooling rack placed on a baking sheet. Reheat the syrup and with a ladle, generously imbibe the cake.
Using the syrup that has pooled onto the baking sheet, imbibe the cake twice more. Allow the cake to cool for a minimum of 12 hours before serving.

Pairs well with
Our *Rose* tea

A CUP OF CAMELLIA?

Did you know that the tea plant comes from the same family as the camellia, the Theaceae.

TEA IS FOR THEA

The father of modern plant names, the Swedish botanist Carl Linnaeus, initially attributed the tea plant to the *Thea* genus. In 1818, the English botanist Robert Sweet shifted all *Thea* into Linnaeus's *Camellia* classification and the name stuck. This evergreen plant has white flowers with five-petals that are smaller but similar to the garden camellia. The earliest known traces of ancient tea plantations discovered in the province of Yunnan date back 6,000 years. Today there exist three varieties of *Camellia sinensis* and more than 500 types of cultivars.

CLIMBING THE TEA MOUNTAIN

The tea plant is at home in tropical and sub-tropical climates and is particularly fond of high-altitudes. The higher you climb, the better the tea in your cup becomes. The rigorous, high-altitude conditions slow tree growth and concentrate flavor into the leaf. To aid harvesting, tree plants are pruned to 4 feet. Tea is also harvested from wild plants, some of which are 2,000 years old and 80 feet tall.

You don't have to live on a mountain however: tea plants are at home in any garden. Plant them in semi-shade and they'll flourish if the soil is acidic or if you use ericaceous fertilizer. Tea-leaves also make for great compost and they contain all the nutrients necessary to grow robust and healthy plants.

Raspberry Passion Fruit Tart

Serves 8 people

Preparation: 1 hour and 20 minutes
Cooking time: 20 minutes
Resting time: minimum of 13 hours + 2 hours minimum for the pastry dough (preferably the evening before)

Passion fruit cream

1 cup + 1 ½ tbsp | 250 g butter
2 sheets of gelatin (½ tbsp | 4 g powdered gelatin)
2 organic eggs + 1 organic egg yolk
¾ cup | 150 g granulated sugar
1 tsp cornstarch (cornflour)
⅔ cup | 125 g passion fruit purée
2 tbsp | 30 ml lemon juice

Sweet almond pastry shell

12 ½ oz | 350 g dough: see Basic Recipe, p. 297
2 ½ tbsp | 20 g all-flour for work surface
1 ½ tbsp | 20 g butter for tart pan

PASSION FRUIT CREAM

1. Prepare the cream a day ahead.
Bring the butter to room temperature to soften.
Soften the sheets of gelatin in very cold water for 10 minutes.
In a bowl, whisk together the eggs, the yolk, the sugar and the cornstarch.
Incorporate the passion fruit puree and lemon juice.
Drain the sheets of gelatin and squeeze hard to remove all excess water.

2. In a saucepan, cook the egg mixture over low heat, stirring with a spatula until it simmers, allowing the cream to thicken. Remove from heat and add the drained gelatin.
Allow to cool slightly for approximately 10 minutes. The cream should be warm but not scalding (less than 140°F | 60°C). Add the softened butter and in a food processor or a blender, blend the butter into the cream until very smooth.
Pour into an airtight container and refrigerate for a minimum of 12 hours until firm.

Garnish

3 ¼ cups | 400 g raspberries

Equipment

Tart pan, 9 ½ inch | 24 cm diameter, ¾ inch | 2 cm high

SWEET ALMOND PASTRY SHELL

3. On a floured work surface, roll the dough out to ¹⁄₁₀ inch | 2 mm thick and press into the buttered pan. Refrigerate for 1 hour.
Preheat the oven to 325° F | 165 °C | gas mark 3.
Meanwhile, using a fork, prick the surface of the dough to keep it from distorting during baking. Fit a round piece of parchment paper over the dough, carefully pressing into the corners and working up the sides so it will stay in place in the oven.
Place dried beans or pie weights on top, spreading them out in an even layer.

4. Bake for approximately 20 minutes until slightly golden. Remove from oven.
Remove dried beans and parchment paper.
If the pastry shell is still pale, return to oven uncovered and finish baking until the shell is colored slightly. Remove from oven and allow to cool.

ASSEMBLY

5. Fill the cooled baked tart shell with passion fruit cream and refrigerate until time to serve.
At the last moment, arrange the raspberries in an attractive pattern across the top.

Pairs well with
Our *Rose* or *Violette* tea

Upside-Down Apple Tart

Makes 8 individual tarts
Preparation: 45 minutes
Cooking time: 2 hours and 15 minutes
Resting time: 3 hours

Tatin apples and caramel
12 apples (Golden if possible)
1 ½ cup | 300 g granulated sugar
9 tbsp | 125 g butter

Caramel
½ cup + 1 tbsp | 100 ml water
1 ½ cup | 300 g granulated sugar
9 tbsp | 125 g butter

Puff pastry top
17 ½ oz | 500 g puff pastry:
see Basic Recipe, p. 298.
2 ½ tbsp | 20 g flour for the work surface

Equipment
8 ramekins, 4 inch | 10 cm diameter
Pastry cutter 5 inch | 13 cm diameter

TATIN APPLES AND CARAMEL

1. Peel, core and cut apples into 3 large slices. Dice butter into small cubes.
In a saucepan, cook ½ cup + 1 tbsp | 100 ml water and sugar until it has a golden caramel color. Remove from heat and immediately add the butter cubes to stop the caramelization. Be careful not to burn yourself. Stand back and stir until the butter is fully incorporated into the caramel.
Pour the caramel into the ramekins to a thickness of $1/5$-inch | 5 mm.
Allow to cool.

2. Preheat the oven to 325°F | 165°C | gas mark 3. Fit the apples into the ramekins as tightly as possible, upright and side by side. The apples should be higher than the ramekin. They will shrink by half when baked. Place in oven and bake for 1 ½ hours Remove from oven and allow to cool.

Pairs well with
Our *Mûre* tea

•••

PUFF PASTRY TOP

3. On a floured work surface, roll out the puff pastry dough. Using a round pastry cutter, cut out 5 inch | 13 cm diameter disks and allow them to rest in the refrigerator for 30 minutes.
Preheat the oven to 325°F | 165°C | gas mark 3.

4. Cover the apples with the rounds of pastry and push down the dough inside the ramekins and around the fruit to keep everything in place when removing from the mold.
Place in oven and bake for 35 minutes. Allow to cool. Place in refrigerator for at least 2 hours for the caramel and the pectin in the apples to set.

5. Heat water in a frying pan. Dip the bottom of the ramekins one at a time in the hot water for 15 seconds. Run the blade of a knife inside each ramekin to loosen the tarts. Press down lightly onto the pastry to push the tart up and unmold on a serving plate, apples facing up.

Chef's tip

When ready to serve, reheat tarts at 250°F | 130°C | gas mark ½ and serve warm with whipped cream. The tarts can also be served with a scoop of vanilla ice cream. The contrast between the hot and the cold is delicious.

SPRING HARVEST

Harvesting tea leaves is an ancestral art. As with vineyards it is vital for the quality of tea.

A SECULAR TRADITION

Harvesting tea is a delicate process and tea is still mainly harvested by hand except in Japan and Georgia where the process is mechanized. Harvesting is a predominantly female profession. With wicker baskets on their backs, equipped with measuring sticks as a guide – only the leaves growing above the stick are harvested. The leaf is dexterously plucked between thumb and forefinger. For the highest grades of tea only the bud is picked; lower grades include 1–3 leaves. Fingernails and mechanical tools are not used to avoid bruising. It is a painstaking meticulous art that, on the most prestigious estates, is passed on from generation to generation.

FEELING FLUSH

Tea plants are harvested several times a year. After dormant periods of fifteen days the tree awakens and "flushes". The first flush in spring brings the best quality leaves with more delicate fragrances than the second and third flushes in summer and autumn.

Meringues

Makes 20–22 meringues
Preparation: 20 minutes
Cooking time: 2 ½ hours

1 cup | 120 g confectioners' (icing) sugar
4 organic egg whites
½ cup + 2 tbsp | 120 g granulated sugar

Equipment
Electric mixer
Piping bag fitted with a ½ inch | 10 mm star tip

1. Preheat the oven to 210°F | 100°C | gas mark ¼. Sift the confectioners' sugar.

2. In a clean, dry bowl, whip the egg whites to a foam using an electric mixer. Once they are frothy, add 3 tbsp | 40 g of granulated sugar and continue to whip until firm. Add another 3 tbsp | 40 g of granulated sugar and whip for 1 minute. Pour in the remaining 3 tbsp | 40 g of granulated sugar and whip for 1 more minute.
With a rubber spatula, gently fold in the sifted confectioners' sugar.

3. Transfer the meringue to the piping bag fitted with a star tip. On a baking sheet lined with parchment paper, pipe twists of meringue. Be sure to leave enough space between meringues as they will spread and rise during baking. If you do not have a piping bag and tip, use two spoons dipped in hot water to shape quenelles (3-sided ovals).

Pairs well with
Our *Mûre* tea

• • •

4. Place sheet in oven and bake for approximately 2 ½ hours.
The meringues should bake slowly and gradually dry out. Watch that they do not darken too quickly. Allow to cool completely and store in an airtight container.

Chef's tip

Dust the tops of meringues with confectioners' sugar and serve with an ice cream or a sorbet.

GARDENS OF WONDER

In 1834, a British civil servant living in Darjeeling in the north-east of India tried planting tea seeds in his garden.

THE THIRST FOR TRADE

To free themselves from their dependency on Chinese production that was hampering their cravings, the British set out to grow their own tea. Within the confines of their Empire they found the perfect terrain and climatic conditions amidst the foothills of the Himalayas. After the botanist Robert Fortune's industrial espionage mission to China, during which he secured the blueprint for cultivating the *Camellia sinensis* plants, the British established their first tea garden, the Tukvar garden, in 1856. Other gardens soon followed and by 1866, there were over forty. Today there are over ninety gardens. This know-how was then exported to Ceylon, present-day Sri Lanka.

BENGAL TEA

Today, the gardens of Darjeeling are known the world over and the most prestigious are on a par with the finest Chinese producers. Harvesting in Darjeeling is no mean feat; some slopes have 70° inclines.
Although Darjeeling tea production is protected with a Geographical Indication tag, there is a large quantity of counterfeit tea on the market and four times more "Darjeeling" tea is sold around the world each year than actually produced.

Russian TEA

Russian Tea

In Russia, a cup of tea is a rich full-bodied tonic evoking long journeys across the frozen steppes and romantic tales of derring-do

GOING IN STRONG

The world's fifth ranked tea consumer, Russia is fond of a powerful, full-flavored cup of tea, with sugar but no milk served with candies, cookies, *baranki* pastries and savory *pirojki* pies. Once upon a time, the time-honored drinking method was to cool the tea in the saucer, place a piece of sugar between the teeth then sup the strong brew through the sugar.

To alleviate the bitterness and provide the sweet taste that Russians still love today, preserves or honey are added to create a hot, comforting, syrupy concoction.

Russians take tea at five o'clock, drinking up to ten or twelve cups per day, and have always drunk it piping hot. According to an old custom, hospitable hosts should offer napkins to visitors unfamiliar with such hot beverages to wipe their perspiring brow. Before tea arrived in Russia, the Slavs were already accustomed to drinking hot infusions of spices

17th century, with the tsarist seal of approval. In 1638, the Mongolian ruler, the Altyn Khan offered the Russian ambassador Vassili Starkov a case of 250 pounds of tea to take back to Tsar Michael I. Starkov initially refused. What was he to do with four chests of dead leaves – an insult in comparison to the mink coats he had conveyed to the prince? The Altyn Khan insisted and dispatched an emissary to the Tsar's court to prepare the beverage. It was an immediate hit. Imperial Russia was enthralled and by 1679, Russia agreed to a treaty with China for regular tea imports by camel caravan in exchange for furs. The difficult trade route limited supply, so during his reign (1682–1725), Peter the Great began construction on the Tea Road through Siberia and tea became a staple import. By 1860, 6,000 tons were arriving in the country by caravan. But despite the arrival of the Trans-Siberian railway, it was still expensive. So in the 19th century, to take control of their internal market, Russians began developing their own plantations in the Caucasian mountains between the Black Sea and the Caspian Sea. By producing black tea themselves they brought down the price and tea consumption rose across the Empire. While Georgian production is still prolific, Chinese, Japanese and Indian teas remain the gold standard in the tea world.

Beet Tartare

Serves 6 people
Preparation: 45 minutes
Cooking time: 10 minutes
Drying time: 2 ½ hours

2 cups | 405 g cooked beets
⅓ cup | 108 ml Greek yogurt
½ tbsp | 6 g fresh mint
Juice of ½ lime
1 tsp | 3 g tahini
1 tbsp | 21 g cream of balsamic vinegar
¾ tbsp | 16 g pomegranate molasses
5 tsp | 25 ml extra virgin olive oil
⅓ tbsp | 6 g table salt

Tapioca crisps
5 ⅓ oz | 150 g tapioca pearls
Frying oil
Salt, pepper

Garnish
1 lime
1 punnet of coriander microgreens

Equipment
Mandoline slicer
Pastry ring, 3 inch | 8 cm in diameter

Ideally, the tapioca crisps should be prepared the day before.

1. Preheat the oven to 205°F | 95°C | gas mark ¼. Place the tapioca pearls and 10 tbsp of water in a hemispherical bowl. Whisk forcefully to crush the pearls. Process the batter in a blender to obtain a smooth batter. Spread the batter on a baking sheet lined with oven-safe plastic wrap or waxed paper and bake for 10 minutes.

2. When the batter is cooked, carefully remove the plastic wrap. Take care not to roll it over itself. When cooked, it is extremely elastic and tends to stick to itself. Place the preparation on a rack and allow to dry in the oven at 150°F | 65°C | gas mark ¼ for 2 ½ hours.
After drying, cut rectangles and fry them in hot oil (356°F | 180°C). Season the crisps as they come out of the oil.

Pairs well with
Our *Othello* tea

3. With the mandoline, grate the cooked beets. Place all the ingredients, except the mint, in a large bowl. Adjust the seasoning.

4. To serve, place the pastry ring in the middle of the plate and fill with the tartare. Place two tapioca chips upright on the tartare. Garnish with minced mint leaves, a sprinkle of coriander and a wedge of lime.

Chef's tip

You can also buy raw beets and cook them yourself. I recommend cooking them in a salt crust to concentrate the flavors. Simply cover the beets with coarse sea salt and place in an oven at 130°C 150°F | 65°C | gas mark ¼ for 1 ½ to 2 hours. Allow beets to cool for at least 30 minutes before rinsing them to remove their skin and the excess salt.

THAT RUSSIAN FLAVOR

There's "Russian tea" and "Russian Tea". One is tea grown in Russia; the other is a rich warming winter brew of tea, citrus flavors and spices.

A TEA FOR TRAVELERS

In the 18th century, when tea-loving Western-Europeans traveled to Russia and discovered Russian tea, they preferred it to what they were used to drinking back home. The better flavor was due to transport. Once upon a time, Chinese tea was conveyed by camel caravan to Russia via Siberia and the Urals, a journey that took six months. Teas imported to western Europe meanwhile arrived by sea in ships' holds so damp that often cargo had to be dried before sale.

A RECIPE FOR REFINEMENT

Russian Tea is also a recipe whereby black tea is sweetened with citrus fruits and spices, a blend which became fashionable in Europe in the 19th century. In 1894, the early lifestyle guru of French savoir-faire, Baroness Staffe, declared: "Refined Russians add apple blossom to their loose leaf tea. The fragrant floral notes blend exquisitely with the finesse of the leaf. The result is intoxicating." A traditional family recipe for Russian Tea would include lemon zests, orange peel, bergamot, and blackcurrants with their leaves.

Salmon Rillettes and Tapioca Chips

Serves 6 people
Preparation: 45 minutes
Cooking time: 10 minutes

9 oz | 250 g raw salmon (ideally certified sea-raised salmon)
3 ½ oz | 100 g sliced, Scottish smoked salmon
3 ⅔ tbsp | 55 g cream cheese
1 bunch of chives
2 ¾ tbsp | 50 ml of freshly squeezed lemon juice
2 ⅓ tsp | 10 ml organic olive oil
1 pinch of Espelette pepper (or hot Paprika)
1 pinch of *fleur de sel* (or other coarse sea salt)

Tapioca crisps
5 ⅓ oz | 150 g green tapioca pearls
Frying oil
Salt, pepper

1. Prepare the tapioca crisps as indicated in the Beet Tartare recipe, p. 182.

2. Prepare the salmon rillettes: slice the raw salmon into small pavés and steam at 203°F | 95°C for 10 minutes. Place in refrigerator.

3. Meanwhile, trim the smoked salmon of dark portions and cut into small cubes. Wash and mince the chives. Whip the cream cheese and add the lemon juice and *fleur de sel*.

4. When the salmon is cold, mash it with a fork and add the smoked salmon, the chives, the cream cheese and the lemon juice. Add olive oil and Espelette pepper. Mix thoroughly to achieve a homogenous spread. Adjust seasoning to taste.

Dill cream (3 ⅕ oz | 90 g)
3 tbsp | 48 g mascarpone
2 ⅓ tbsp | 35 ml heavy (double) cream
1 handful of baby spinach
½ bunch of dill
1 pinch of table salt

Garnish
1 bunch of flat leaf micro-parlsey
½ lime

5. Prepare the dill cream: bring a pan of water to a boil. Plunge the dill and spinach in the boiling water. When the water begins to boil again, wait for 30 seconds. Drain immediately and blend to obtain a smooth purée. Place the mascarpone and cream in a bowl and whisk with a hand held mixer. Add the dill-spinach purée and a dash of salt. Continue to whisk the cream. Add a small amount of the cream to the salmon rillettes to lighten the texture.

6. To serve, place a quenelle of salmon rillettes on the plate and garnish with the dill cream. Place the tapioca chips upright on the cream. Add a few dots of cream around the plate and finish with a sprinkle the parsley microgreens and a slice of lime.

Pairs well with
Our *Othello* tea

French Toast – Traditional and Rose-flavored

Serves 6 people
Preparation: 25 minutes
Cooking time: 5 minutes
Refrigeration : 8 hours

1 round (mousseline) brioche (8 inch | 20 cm tall)
1 ½ tbsp | 15 g butter for the frying pan

Batter

1 ⅔ cups | 400 ml heavy (double) cream
½ cup + 2 tbsp | 115 g granulated sugar
4 organic egg yolks
½ a vanilla pod

1. With a sharp knife, slice the vanilla pod half lengthwise. Using the tip, scrape the interior to remove the seeds. Pour the cream into a saucepan, add the vanilla pod and seeds and bring to a simmer. Remove from heat, cover and allow to infuse for 1 hour until completely cool.

2. In a large bowl, whisk the egg yolks and granulated sugar until the mixture starts to pale. Strain the cream mixture, bring it back to a slow boil and then pour it over the egg and sugar mixture. Mix well and refrigerate for at least 8 hours.

3. Cut the brioche into ¾ inch | 2.5 cm thick slices.

4. Dip each slice quickly on both sides into the cream mixture. Heat a knob of butter in a hot pan before placing the slices of soaked brioche. Turn them over regularly and keep a careful eye on the brioche, which burns easily. Serve hot.

Variation rose-flavored French toast

Starting with plain French toast, add a small ramekin of rose-flavored whipped cream, raspberry coulis and a few fresh raspberries.

Rose-flavored whipped cream
1 cup | 250 ml heavy (double) cream
2 ½ tbsp | 20 g confectioners' (icing) sugar
⅔ tsp | 5 ml rose syrup

Raspberry Coulis
1 cup | 150 g fresh raspberries (or crumbled frozen raspberries)
2 ½ tsp | 10 g granulated sugar (to taste depending on the tartness of your raspberries)

1. In the bowl of an electric mixer (or with a whisk), whisk the cream (the colder it is, the better it whips), the confectioners' sugar and the rose syrup until the whipped cream is light and forms peaks. Keep refrigerated until the last moment.

2. For the coulis, crush the raspberries. Add sugar and mix. Strain through a fine meshed sieve. Keep cold in the refrigerator.

Pairs well with
Our *Mathilde* tea

ALL WORSHIP THE SAMOVAR

Although also used in Turkey, Iran, Azerbaijan and Morocco, the samovar is the symbol of the great Russian tea tradition.

THE TULA TRADEMARK
After the first samovars appeared in the 17th century, Tula, to the south of Moscow, became the prestigious home of their manufacture and prior to the Great War, the city produced 660,000 samovars per year. Such is the city's renown for its samovar output, the Russians have an expression, "travel to Tula with your own samovar" which has the same meaning as "to take coals to Newcastle". Today Tula is still the center for samovar manufacture.

THE SOUL OF THE HOME
The samovar has an ingenious self-boiler system: the burning charcoal in the base of the boiler heats water in the lower chamber. The teapot sits on top of the boiler which maintains it at the right temperature. The tea in the teapot is steeped to obtain a strong concentrate. This concentrate is served in cups into which hot water may be added from the tap below. The samovar is the soul of the home. It has important cameo roles in Chekhov plays and is a key feature of Pushkin and Tolstoy novels. Even though it is often replaced by electric devices today, the samovar remains the symbol of Russian hospitality.

Crêpes

Makes 20 crêpes
Preparation: 20 minutes
Cooking time: 3 minutes per crêpe
Resting time: minimum of 1 hour

1 orange, unwaxed
1⅓ cups | 165 g cake (SR) flour
3 tbsp | 40 g granulated sugar
4 organic eggs
2 cups + 2 tbsp | 500 ml whole milk
3 tbsp | 40 g butter +
1 ½ tbsp | 20 g for the frying pan
1 tbsp oil
1 tbsp rum (optional)
1 tbsp Cointreau or Grand Marnier (optional)

1. Using a grater, zest the orange.
Sift the flour into a large bowl. Add sugar, grated orange zest and eggs. Gradually add the milk while whisking constantly to obtain a smooth batter with no lumps. In a small saucepan, melt the butter. Add to the batter along with the oil and alcohols if desired.
Allow the batter to rest for at least 1 hour at room temperature.

2. Heat a frying pan (preferably non-stick) over a moderate heat and lightly butter the surface with a paper towel. Ladle just enough batter to cover the surface of the hot pan, tilting it to form a thin, even layer. Leave to cook until the batter has firmed up (less than a minute).
Flip the crêpe over and cook until the other side is lightly golden.

Pairs well with
Our *Mathilde* tea

• • •

Stack the crêpes as you go to keep them moist. If you have two pans, you can fill one crêpe while cooking the other.

3. Sprinkle crêpes with confectioners' sugar or top with low-sugar jam, melted chocolate, or a chocolate hazelnut spread.

Chef's tip

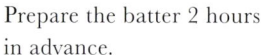

Prepare the batter 2 hours in advance.
If there are lumps in your batter, blend with a hand held blender or mixer as briefly as possible – just enough to eliminate the lumps but not enough for the batter to froth.
If you are cooking the crêpes in advance, stack them to keep them moist.
Keep them stacked at room temperature.

Gingerbread

Serves 8 to 10 people
Preparation: 1 ½ hours
Cooking time: 55 minutes
Resting time: 12 hours + 24 hours

⅔ cup | 150 ml water
⅓ oz | 10 g star anise or wild anise
5 tbsp | 75 g butter +
1 ½ tbsp | 20 g for the loaf pan
½ cup | 100 g granulated sugar
⅓ cup | 100 g chestnut honey
1 orange, unwaxed
1 lemon, unwaxed
1 cup | 110 g rye flour
1 cup | 130 g all-purpose flour
(reserve 1 tbsp | 10 g for loaf pan)
1 ½ tsp | 6 g baking powder
2 tsp | 5 g ground cinnamon
1 tsp | 3 g ground gingerbread spice mix
2 tbsp | 30 g candied orange, diced

Equipment
Loaf pan, 10 x 3 x 3 inch | 25 x 8 x 8 cm
Grater

1. Ideally, begin the recipe the day before to allow the liquid mixture to cool completely.
In a small saucepan, bring ⅔ cup | 150 ml water, star anise, butter, sugar, and honey to a boil. Remove from heat, cover and allow to infuse for 2 hours. Strain with a fine mesh sieve and discard solids.
Allow to cool at room temperature overnight.

2. The following day, butter the loaf pan and line the bottom with a long rectangle of parchment paper to make unmolding easier. Refrigerate the pan 10 minutes until the butter hardens. Remove and dust the interior with flour.
Turn the pan upside down and lightly tap out any excess flour.

3. Grate the orange and lemon zests.

Pairs well with
Our *Jour de fête* tea

• • •

In a large bowl, sift together both flours, baking powder and spices.
Add the grated zests and the diced candied orange. Slowly pour the cooled infused liquid over the dry mixture and stir with a wooden spatula (as for a crêpe batter) until the batter is smooth.

4. Preheat oven to 410°F | 210°C | gas mark 6.
Fill the loaf pan with gingerbread batter, to ¾ inch | 2 cm below the rim.
Bake for 10 minutes. Remove from oven and slit the top crust lengthwise with a sharp knife.
Immediately return the cake to the oven and lower the temperature 350°F | 180°C | gas mark 4. Bake for 45 minutes. Check to see if the cake is done by inserting the tip of a knife into the center. The knife should come out dry and clean, with no traces.

5. Remove the gingerbread cake from the oven and allow to cool for 5 minutes.
Unmold onto a rack and let cool completely.

Chef's tip

Once completely cool, wrap the cake in plastic wrap and leave at room temperature for 24 hours before serving.

FROM RUSSIA WITH LOVE

Served in magnificent decorative porcelain services, the Russian tea ritual, with its lavish spread of candies and cookies and rich intoxicating brew, is steeped in Russian folklore.

LOMONOSOV PORCELAIN

To compete with the Chinese and Europeans, the Russian tsar Peter the Great was eager to produce homespun Russian porcelain. To this end, in 1744, his daughter Empress Elisabeth founded the imperial porcelain manufactory of Saint-Petersburg to serve "native trade and native art", while a gifted Russian mining engineer Dimitri Vinogradov (1720–1758) perfected the Russian formula for hard-paste porcelain. The reputation of the Imperial Porcelain Manufactory grew and the Romanovs commissioned exquisite pieces. The manufactory's trademark cobalt net design highlighted with 22 carat gold, is based on the service fashioned for Catherine the Great. In 1925, on the occasion of the 200th anniversary of the Russian Academy of Science, it was given the name of the academy's founder, Mikhail Lomonosov.

TABLE MANNERS

Russian tea time is a heart-warming ritual; the table is a feast for the eyes and hungry mouths. Amid the shimmering, exquisitely sculpted cobalt-blue, gold-laced porcelain sit mountains of fresh fruit, confectionery, fruit jelly, butter cookies, and savory *pirojki* pies. This tea moment is a festive affair, and a vital part of Russian daily life.

TEA and Travel

...

Photographs produced at the Ladurée Bonaparte Tearoom in Paris, decorated by Roxane Rodriguez

Tea and Travel

*Without travelers, tea would never have made it west.
Thanks to the intrepid journeys of bare-footed Buddhist monks and
audacious adventurers, the leaf left its homestead to travel the world.*

TEA'S MAIDEN VOYAGE

It was Buddhist monks who took tea plants on their first journey from China to Japan. According to legend in the 9th century, the first tea garden was the work of the Japanese monk Saichō who introduced Chinese tea to southern Japan. In the West, the plant was still unknown and it was not until the golden age of discovery when fearless explorers such as Marco Polo (1254–1324) traveled east and wrote their observations in their journals that Europe gradually came to learn about the drink. Portuguese sailors and Jesuit missionaries braved the Indian Ocean and China Sea to imbibe the Zen ambrosia themselves and recorded its role in daily life and its beneficial effects.

In 1610, the first cargo of tea arrived in Europe, conveyed by the Dutch East India Company, while tea also made its way into Russia via camel caravan along the Silk Road.

THE TEA RACE

Tea soon won over the hearts and palates of English, French and Dutch courtiers and noblemen thrilled to get a taste of the world without leaving their bedchambers. Despite the high price of tea, Amsterdam, London and Paris took to the brew and its trade became ferociously competitive. The ensuing trade war was finally won by the British who monopolized the Chinese supply. Tea provided a lucrative form for taxation, and as taxes rose so did the illegal trade in tea.

In the 19th century, China was still a treacherous ten-month trail from Europe. However, in the 1830s, America unveiled the tea clipper, a faster sleeker craft, which revolutionized transport and cut journey times by up to a third. Each year, English captains vied to win the race to bring the first spring harvest back safe and sound to London in less than three months.

In the 1870s the elegant clipper was replaced by steam boats, which, while not necessarily faster, were more solid. The completion of the Suez Canal in 1869 also brought a new time advantage.

TEA –
THE WORLD TOUR

Under European impetus, tea plantations spread beyond China and Japan. The Dutch started growing tea in Indonesia from the late 17th century. During the 19th century, India and Ceylon began exporting to the British Empire. In Malawi, South Africa, Cameroon, Uganda and Kenya, ravenous colonial thirst spurred tea culture onwards.

North Africa has its own story, where it seems mint tea has been deeply embedded in daily rituals since time immemorial. Mint tea however is a relatively recent institution which only became established in the 19th century. Chinese tea was already being imported into the court of the Moroccan Sultan, Moulay Ismaïl three centuries before, but remained the Sultan's exclusive secret pleasure, until the global tea trade missionaries, the British, intervened. Access to the

Baltic states was blockaded during the Crimean War. So the East India Company decided to unload their surplus tea on the Maghreb via the trading posts of Tangiers and Mogador (today's Essaouira). The new arrival fitted seamlessly into local life – people were already drinking fresh mint leaves in infusions and green tea helped alleviate the bitterness. In half-a-century, mint tea conquered Morocco and the Sahara.

Falafels

Serves 6 people
Preparation: 45 minutes
Cooking time: 15 minutes

Falafels

1 cup + 2 ½ tbsp | 150 g roasted chick pea flour
1 ¾ cup | 500 ml whole milk
7 tbsp | 100 g salted butter
2 ¾ tbsp | 50 ml soy sauce
5 ½ tbsp | 100 ml sesame oil
¾ oz | 20 g coriander leaves
2 ½ tsp | 5 g ground fennel seeds
1 tsp | 2 g ground cumin
2 pinches of table salt

Breadcrumb coating

2 cups | 250 g flour
2 organic eggs
1 ¾ cup | 200 g Panko breadcrumbs
Frying oil

1. Ideally, drain the cottage cheese in a clean cloth the day before.

2. Beat the milk and roasted chick pea flour together briskly to avoid clumps. Put the mixture in a saucepan over low heat and cook for approximately 15 minutes.

3. Take the batter off the heat and add the butter, soy sauce, ground fennel seed, sesame oil, chopped coriander, ground cumin and salt. Spread the mixture in a baking sheet and cover with plastic wrap. When cool, make small balls with a spoon.

4. Dredge each ball in flour, beaten egg and Panko crumbs, in that order. Dredge the balls again but this time only in the beaten egg and Panko crumbs. Place the falafels in the refrigerator while you prepare the sauce.

Falafel sauce

½ cup | 100 g low-fat cottage cheese
3 tbsp | 50 ml sesame oil
5 sprigs of coriander, leaves only
Juice of ½ a lime
2 pinches of ground Espelette pepper
(or hot Paprika)
Table salt

Garnish

½ romaine lettuce

Equipment

Deep fryer

5. The sauce: mix the drained cottage cheese with sesame oil, lime juice, Espelette pepper, salt and minced coriander leaves. Adjust seasoning.

6. Heat the deep fryer to 350°F | 180°C.
Fry the falafels a few at a time until evenly brown on all sides. Drain on paper towels. Accompany them with crispy romaine leaves and a well-chilled sauce.

Pairs well with
Our *Ceylan* tea

TAKING CARE OF TEA

It might seem that dried tea leaves with their 3% water content can last forever. Be careful, tea is not immortal.

NOT FOR ETERNI-TEA
Stored for too long in poor conditions, tea loses its aromatic qualities, so proper storage conditions are essential. Tea is a sensitive animal: to protect it from its enemies – light, heat, damp and air – it likes sealed, non-transparent containers. Light and heat dry the leaves which then lose their volatile color and aroma molecules. Fermentation in tea is stopped at the right moment to attain the right balance and exposure to air encourages further unwanted oxidation; in the process, aroma molecules are transformed and lose their intensity. Tea is also liable to absorb odors and humidity.

FRESH OR AGED
Only one tea improves with age: the black tea, Pu Erh. All others change over time, some faster than others. The most delicate are green teas that should be consumed when fresh. Then come the spring Darjeelings and semi-fermented teas. Generally the more oxidized or fermented a tea is, the better it keeps.

Avocado Slices

Serves 6 people
Preparation: 30 minutes

3 avocados
3 sheets of nori
3 tbsp | 50 ml toasted sesame oil
2 tbsp | 20 g brown flax seeds
2 tbsp | 20 g golden flax seeds
Juice of ½ lime
1 punnet of red shiso microgreens
2 slices of sourdough bread
Olive oil
Ground Espelette pepper
(or hot Paprika)
Fleur de sel (or other coarse sea salt)

1. Slice the avocados in two lengthwise and remove the pit. With a spoon, scoop out the flesh neatly. Slice the avocados evenly.

2. In a frying pan, toast the brown and golden flax seeds with a drop of olive oil. The seeds will puff. Dry the 2 slices of bread in the oven. When they are dry and crispy, crumble them.

3. Roll the nori sheets and snip thin strips with a pair of scissors. Pour a little puddle of grilled sesame oil onto the bottom of a plate. Add a squeeze of lime juice. Arrange the avocado slices on top and sprinkle with the flax seeds and bread crumbs. Season with the *fleur de sel* and the ground Espelette pepper. Sprinkle a few nori strips and some red shiso microgreens.

Pairs well with
Our *Mille et Une Nuits* or *Ceylan* tea

Cinnamon Raisin Buns

Makes 15 buns
Preparation: 2 hours
Cooking time: 20–30 minutes
Resting time: 4 ½–5 ½ hours

5 ½ cups | 500 g cake (SR) flour
2 cups | 200 g unsalted butter
4 organic eggs
3 tbsp | 35 g granulated sugar
3 ½ tbsp | 25 g powdered milk
4 ½ tbsp | 38 g fresh baker's yeast
1 tsp | 6 g *fleur de sel* (or other coarse sea salt)

Garniture
1 ¼ cup | 125 g pastry cream (see recipe p. 302)
3 ½ tbsp | 50 g unsalted butter (creamed)
1 cup | 100 g ground almonds (almond flour)
2 tbsp | 15 g ground cinnamon
1 cup | 150 g golden seedless raisins (sultanas)

1. Prepare the dough: in the bowl of a stand mixer fitted with a dough hook, place the flour, sugar, powdered milk and salt. Add the yeast dissolved in 12 tbsp | 180 ml water. Mix for 3 to 4 minutes before adding the eggs one at a time. Knead well until the dough is smooth and is no longer sticky.

Form the dough into a ball and leave in the mixing bowl. Cover with plastic wrap and allow to rise for 1 to 2 hours at room temperature (preferably near a heater or in a warm room) until it has doubled in size.

2. Meanwhile, prepare the pastry cream as explained on p. 301. Prepare the filling: bring 2 cups | 500 ml of water to a boil and add the raisins. Allow to swell for approximately 30 minutes, then drain.
Whisk the pastry cream until smooth. Add the creamed butter and whisk again until smooth. Add the almond flour and powdered cinnamon. Finish by gently folding in the cooled raisins.

Equipment
Stand mixer
Plastic wrap

3. Take the dough out of the mixing bowl and quickly knead it with your hands. Stretch out into a rectangle ⅕ inch | 5 mm thick. Butter ⅔ of the dough with 200 g of softened butter with the tips of your fingers (or a dough scraper). Fold the rectangle in thirds (like a business letter) and allow to rest in the refrigerator for 30 minutes. Stretch the dough out again and repeat the butter/folding process. Allow to rest in the refrigerator for 1 hour.

4. Stretch the dough into a short, wide rectangle ⅕ inch | 5 mm thick. Spread the filling across all the dough, leaving a ⅓ inch | 1 cm strip at the top of the rectangle. Roll the dough up into a log (not too tight) towards the clean strip. Lightly dampen the clean strip with a little bit of water and close the log, pressing lightly to fully seal the log. Allow to rest in the refrigerator for 1 hour.

5. Cut the log into 1 inch | 3 cm thick slices and place them on a baking sheet lined with parchment paper. Allow the buns to rise near a source of heat (for example, a radiator) for approximately 1 hour.

6. Preheat the oven to 350°F | 180° C | gas mark 4. Place the buns in the oven and bake for 20 to 30 minutes until they are golden brown.

Pairs well with
Our *Vanille* tea

BLACK TEA VS. GREEN TEA: THE SAME OR DIFFERENT?

Black tea and green tea were long believed to be different species. But what do they have in common?

LET'S ASK A BOTANIST
The work of Scottish botanist Robert Fortune (1812–1880) was crucial to the development of tea in India. By his own admission, his famous horticultural espionage mission to infiltrate Chinese tea plantations was motivated by this question: "The aim of my visit to Foo-Chow-Foo was to infiltrate tea plantations to obtain material proof that black teas are made with leaves from the same tree bearing green tea in the north. I was deeply convinced of this, but I wished to witness it with my own eyes." He also observed how different colors and flavors were obtained from the leaves of a single species, *Camellia sinensis*, and how this difference was due to the way the leaves were processed.

GREEN TEA: A LATE ARRIVAL
Unaware of how tea came to be tea, the West began by drinking black tea. It is possible that initially green tea was imported but that it oxidized on the long grueling journey by sea. It is also possible traders believed oxidized leaves more suitable for surviving the long months on the ocean waves. Either way, the leaves imparted a flavor that was everyone's cup of tea.

Bostocks and Maple Syrup

Makes 8 bostocks
Preparation: 50 minutes
Cooking time: 12 minutes

1 round (mousseline) brioche,
8 inches | 20 cm high
Dark aged rum

Syrup

1 ½ cup | 300 g granulated sugar
1 oz | 30 g ground almonds (almond flour)
1 ½ tbsp | 20 ml orange blossom water

Almond cream

¾ cup | 180 g unsalted butter
1 ½ cup | 200 g confectioners' (icing) sugar
+ 2 ½ tbsp | 20 g for the garnish
2 cups | 200 g ground almonds (almond flour)
1 ½ tbsp | 16 g cornstarch (cornflour)
2 organic eggs
½ cup | 50 g flaked almonds

1. Syrup: In a saucepan, bring ¾ cup | 250 ml of water and the sugar to a boil. Remove from heat and add almond flour. Allow to cool before adding orange blossom water.

2. Almond cream: dice the butter into small cubes and put in a large, heatproof bowl. Place over a pan of gently simmering water to soften until creamy without allowing it to melt. Incorporate the following ingredients in the listed order, making sure to mix well after each addition: confectioners' sugar, almond flour, cornstarch, eggs. Transfer to the piping bag.

3. Preheat the oven to 325°F | 165°C | gas mark 3. Place the brioche on the work surface and cut 8 slices, each ¾ inch | 2.5 cm thick. Warm the syrup and pour into a large bowl. Dip both sides of the brioche slices into the warm syrup. Place on rack to drain. Lightly splash with dark rum.

Pairs well with
Our *Fleur d'Oranger* tea

Equipment
Piping bag fitted with a ½ inch | 10 mm plain tip

4. With the piping bag fitted with its tip, cover each slice with a thin layer of cream (1/10 inch | 2 mm). Sprinkle with flaked almonds.
Place bostocks on a baking sheet lined with parchment paper and bake for approximately 12 minutes. Allow to cool completely, and then dust with confectioners' sugar.

Chef's tip

The older the brioche, the easier it is to soak it. Use the same method as for French toast (recipe p. 190)

Palmiers

Makes 10 biscuits
Preparation: 2 hours
Cooking time: 15–20 minutes
Resting time: 9 ½ hours and 20 minutes

Détrempe
2 ⅓ cups | 290 g all-purpose flour
1 ⅔ cups | 375 g butter
2 tsp | 10 g salt
1 tbsp white vinegar

Butter - flour
1 cup + 3 tbsp | 150 g all-purpose flour
4 tbsp | 60 g butter, diced
½ cup | 100 g granulated sugar

Equipment
Stand mixer
Plastic wrap
Rolling pin

THE *DÉTREMPE*

1. Melt butter and allow to cool. In the bowl of your stand mixer, pour ½ cup + 5 tbsp | 200 ml water, vinegar and salt. When the salt has dissolved, add the flour, then the cooled liquid butter. Knead at slow speed until the *détrempe* is smooth. Carefully wrap in plastic wrap and refrigerate for a minimum of 2 hours.

BUTTER-FLOUR

2. Fit the stand mixer with the paddle attachment. Mix the butter and flour until the mixture is homogeneous. Wrap carefully in plastic wrap and refrigerate for a minimum of 2 hours.

3. On a floured work surface, use a rolling pin to roll out the *détrempe* into a smallish rectangle. Remove from work surface. Roll out the butter-flour mixture into a rectangle twice the size of the *détrempe*. Place the *détrempe* on top of the butter-flour rectangle and fold the butter-flour over the *détrempe* until the latter is completely encased. Smooth out the joins with your hands. Carefully wrap the package in plastic wrap and refrigerate for a minimum of 2 hours.

4. Flour the work surface again and roll out the dough into a wide rectangle that is ⅓-inch | 7 to 8 mm thick.

THE *TOURAGE* (FOLDING)

5. Fold the rectangle onto itself in thirds: take the left third and fold over the middle third. Then take the right third and fold it over the other two. Give the dough a ¼ turn (to the right for example). Remember which sides are folded first and the direction of each turn. The success of the resulting dough will depend on this!

6. Repeat the process. Roll out the dough; fold the rectangle in thirds onto itself. Carefully wrap the dough in plastic wrap. Refrigerate for a minimum of 1 ½ hours. You have completed 2 turns.

Pairs well with
Our *Vanille* tea

7. Repeat steps 5 and 6 (the *tourage*), making sure to use the same sides and turn in the same direction as before! Wrap the dough carefully in plastic wrap and refrigerate for 2 hours.

THE PALMIERS

8. Roll the dough out into a rectangle 1/5-inch | 5 mm thick. Sprinkle the entire surface with granulated sugar and press lightly to ensure the sugar sticks.

9. Roll each long side of the rectangle towards the center. Ensure both sides are approximately the same size. Refrigerate for a minimum of 20 minutes to firm up the dough.

10. Preheat the oven to 350°F | 180° C | gas mark 4. Line a baking sheet with parchment paper. With a very sharp knife, cut slices 1/3 inch | 1 cm thick. Place each palmier on the baking sheet, leaving ample room between each. Place in oven and bake for 15–20 minutes until the palmiers are golden.

Cinnamon Hazelnut Shortbread

Makes 25–30 shortbread biscuits
Preparation: 35 minutes
Cooking time: 15 minutes
Resting time: minimum of 2 hours

1 ¾ cups + 2 tbsp | 170 g cake (SR) flour +
2 ½ tbsp | 20 g for the work surface
½ cup + 2 tbsp | 150 g butter
1 cup + 6 ½ tbsp | 120 g ground hazelnuts
5 tbsp | 50 g chopped, roasted hazelnuts
5 tbsp | 40 g confectioners' (icing) sugar
1 organic egg
1 pinch of ground cinnamon
1 pinch of *fleur de sel* (or other coarse sea salt)

Equipment

Round pastry cutter, 2 ⅓ inch | 6 cm diameter
Plastic wrap (clingfilm)

The dough should ideally be prepared the night before; it will be easier to roll out.

1. Cut the butter into small pieces and put in a large bowl. Work the butter into a cream then add the following ingredients one after the other, making sure to blend well after each addition: *fleur de sel*, cinnamon, confectioners' sugar, ground hazelnuts, chopped hazelnuts, egg and lastly flour.

This can also be done with a stand mixer fitted with the paddle attachment.
Work the dough only enough to bring it together. This will give the biscuits their desired crumbly texture.

2. Roll the dough into a ball and wrap in plastic wrap. Place in the refrigerator for several hours before using.

Pairs well with
Our *Mille et Une Nuits* tea

•••

3. Preheat the oven to 325°F | 165 C | gas mark 3. On a floured work surface, use a rolling pin to roll the dough out to approximately 1/10 inch | 2 mm thick.
Using the pastry cutter, cut out as many disks as you can and place in rows on a baking sheet lined with parchment paper.
Place in oven and bake for 15 minutes until golden. Allow the biscuits to cool completely before serving.

Chef's tip

For anise-almond cookies, replace the hazelnuts with the same quantity of whole almonds. Replace the cinnamon with half as much ground green anise.

HOLY SMOKE!

How did tea come to be smoked? A chance discovery or a cunning ploy to resist foreign invaders?

A SLY MOVE
Smoked tea is produced much like salmon: black tea leaves are smoked in bamboo baskets over smoldering pinewood. Like black tea, smoked tea is possibly the fruit of a chance discovery lost in the mists of time. According to legend, to protect their tea crop from being requisitioned by the army, villagers of Tong Mu set fires to accelerate the drying process and spirit away their harvest. The leaves indeed dried faster but developed a smoky aroma, which unexpectedly appealed to a passing foreign trader who imported the smoked tea to Europe with great success.

NOT ASIA'S CUP OF TEA
A different story however relates how Lapsang Souchong producers used the method to dry leaves, having fallen behind on their delivery schedule to the English. Among other smoked teas, you'll find Tarry Souchong which has a smokier tang than Lapsang and smoked fragrant teas whose aromas are greatly appreciated in Europe. In Asia, people seldom drink smoked tea.

TEA in Love
...

Tea in Love

In his early social comedy, Love in Several Masques, *the novelist and dramatist Henry Fielding scored a society hit with the line: "Love and scandal are the best sweeteners of tea." Two and a half centuries later his words still ring true today.*

TEA FOR TWO

As Doris Day sings in the title song of David Butler's movie *Tea for Two* (1950), tea is: "A hymn to love, the perfect beverage for happiness." The song resonates with the joy and excitement of young love, which is probably why it has been covered so often, notably by Frank Sinatra and Ella Fitzgerald. The chorus – "Picture you upon my knee, just tea for two and two for tea, just me for you, alone…" – has become a recipe for happiness itself.

In love stories, tea brings people together. In David Lean's *Brief Encounter* (1945), it provides the respectable backdrop to the pair's burgeoning infidelity, until even taking tea together becomes compromising. In Vincente Minelli's film, *Tea and Sympathy* (1956), as she tries to reach out to the scorned and friendless Tom, Laura invites him to tea. During these innocent interludes, she gradually falls in love with him. Amid the innocent chink of porcelain, tea is also a moment of complicity. As cup follows cup, who knows where things might lead?

Tea granted moviemakers the perfect storytelling device to sidestep censorship in the early to mid 20th century. Tea and its conventions allow tensions to be expressed while reining in their underlying passions. Beyond the cups and saucers, moviegoers were invited to imagine the more carnal pleasures that might ensue.

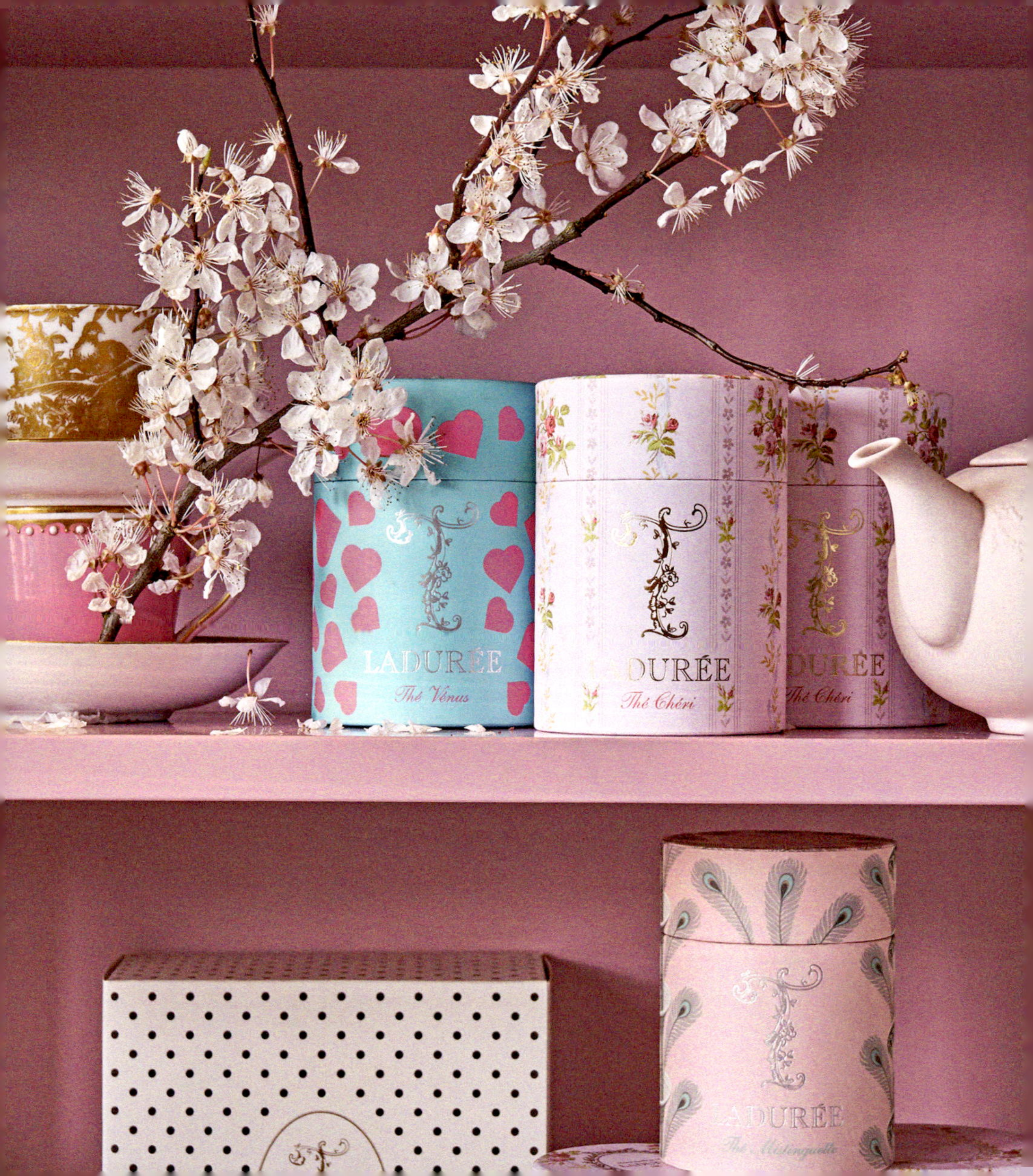
LADURÉE
Thé Vénus
LADURÉE
Thé Chéri
LADURÉE

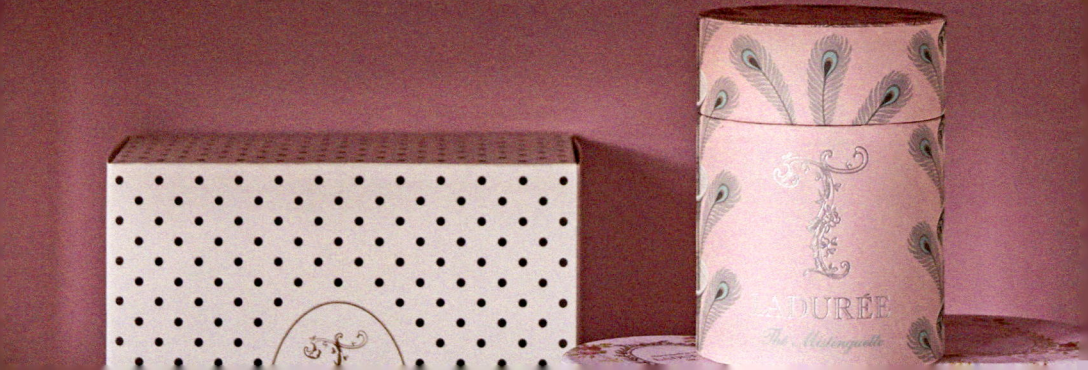

THE ELIXIR OF LOVE

Sharing a cup of tea is an acceptable social convention. It provides the perfect scenario for deeper feelings to take form and flourish, one which writers have also enjoyed exploring. In *Swann's Way* (1913), Marcel Proust takes great pleasure in describing the love burgeoning between his protagonists beneath the innocent veil of the tea-time ritual. Swann and Odette are greatly moved by the small attentions each pays the other during this moment of communion: "She poured out Swann's tea, inquired 'Lemon or milk?' and, on his answering 'Milk, please,' went on, smiling, 'A cloud!' And as he pronounced it excellent, 'You see, I know just how you like it.' This tea had indeed seemed to Swann, just as it seemed to her, something precious, […] all the way home, sitting bolt upright in his brougham, unable to repress the happiness with which the afternoon's adventure had filled him,

he kept on repeating to himself: "What fun it would be to have a little woman like that in a place where one could always be certain of finding, what one never can be certain of finding, a really good cup of tea." (Marcel Proust, *Swann's Way*).

LEMON OR CREAM?

In his novel *Belle du Seigneur* (1968), Albert Cohen offers a different take on Proust's famous scene. The first time Ariane and Solal take tea together, their feelings instantly crystallize: "Her lips trembling, she asked if he'd like a cup of tea. His acquiescence was indifferent. Her cheeks flaming, her stiff hands lifted the pot and poured tea onto the table, into the saucers and finally into the cups.

She apologized and handed him a jug of cream and a plate of sliced lemon. 'Linen or silk?' she asked. He laughed and she looked at him. He smiled and her arms reached out. He took her hands and dropped to one knee. She too knelt before him with such noblesse that she knocked over the teapot, cups, milk jug and lemon slices."

ALL FROM A CUP OF TEA

For true believers, tea is a heady elixir of love, an intoxicating potion of emotions that has long seduced writers providing grist for their mill. In France one of the most famous literary tea times, is Marcel Proust's "madeleine" moment in his work *Remembrance of Things Past*. "I raised to my lips a spoonful of the tea in which I had soaked a morsel of the cake. No sooner had the warm liquid, and the crumbs with it, touched my palate, than a shudder ran through my whole body, and I stopped, intent upon the extraordinary changes that were taking place." In the novel, Proust uses tea time to explore the difference between voluntary and involuntary memory. While the mind can retrieve memory by conscious effort it never captures the essence of the past. Tea time is a moment that encapsulates this essence, a moment of grace and ecstasy in which tea itself is the magic potion, powerful enough to summon the beauty of the past in a simple teaspoon: "The whole of [my childhood village] Combray and of its surroundings took their proper shapes and, growing solid, sprang into being, town and gardens alike, all from my cup of tea."

Salmon Filet

Serves 6 people
Preparation: 30 minutes
Resting time: 20 minutes
Cooking time (blinis): 15 minutes

1 lb | 450 g smoked salmon filet
1 punnet of purple butterfly sorrel leaves (YKA leaves)
1 lime

Blini batter (for 30 small blinis or 12 large ones)
1 cup | 125 g all purpose flour
1 ⅓ cup | 125 g cake (SR) flour
1 bottle of blond or golden ale (330 ml)
1 organic egg white
1 pinch of table salt

Dill cream (1 ¾ oz | 50 g)
3 ½ tbsp | 25 g mascarpone
1 ¼ tbsp | 17 ml heavy (double) cream
1 handful of baby spinach
½ bunch of dill
1 pinch of table salt

1. Prepare the blini batter: in a large bowl, mix flour and salt. Add the ale slowly to prevent lumps. Allow to rest for 20 minutes. Beat the egg whites until stiff. Gently fold them into the batter.

2. Prepare the dill cream: bring a pan of water to a boil. Plunge the dill and spinach in the boiling water. When the water begins to boil again, wait for 30 seconds. Drain immediately and blend to obtain a smooth purée. Place the mascarpone and cream in a bowl and whisk with a hand held mixer. Add the dill-spinach purée and a dash of salt. Place the cream in the piping bag fitted with its tip.

3. Slice the smoked salmon fillet in half lengthwise and cut even slices ⅕ inch | 5 mm thick.

Equipment

Piping bag fitted with a plain tip, ⅕ inch | 6 mm in diameter
Tart ring, 4 ⅓ inch | 11 cm in diameter

4. Place the ring on the plate. Evenly arrange the slices of salmon (2 ⅔ oz | 75 g per person) inside the ring, making sure there are no gaps. Pipe dots of dill cream on the salmon slices. Zest the lime. Garnish with zests and several leaves of purple butterfly leaf sorrel. Remove the ring.

5. Prepare the blinis: heat a non-stick frying pan over a medium flame. With a spoon, shape 5 small mounds of batter, leaving sufficient space between each. After approximately 5 minutes, flip each blini over and cook for an additional 5 minutes. Remove the blinis from the frying pan and keep them warm while cooking the others. Cut each blini in half and arrange them carefully.

Pairs well with

Our *Lapsang Souchon* tea

EACH TO THEIR OWN TEA

Today, more than ever, taking tea is a moment of mutual pleasure and of attention to others.

LOVE AND FRIENDSHIP
"A tea ceremony is a coming together in feeling, a meeting of good comrades in a good season." Yasunari Kawabata (1899–1972). Japanese and Chinese tea-houses serve this social purpose.

PERSONALI-TEA
Tea for two, three, four or more offers the perfect pretext for discovery, a chance to taste new teas, share rare leaves and appreciate their subtle flavors. Tasting is a social pastime. As with wine, finding the right tea for the right dish is entertaining. Every tea has its moment, every person their own "tea-temperament", the *cuppa* that corresponds best to personality.
At formal gatherings, classic favorites such as Earl Grey or Darjeeling always go down well. Yoga aficionados and more meditative friends will appreciate Japanese green tea. Kids will go for fruit, caramel or vanilla teas, while coffee-lovers can often be tempted by stronger smoked teas, such as Lapsang Souchong. For those amorous interludes, why not try something surprising like Oolong with orange blossom or a sensuous Yunnan?

Croque-madame

Serves 6 people
Preparation: 50 minutes
Cooking time: 18 minutes

6 packages of puff pastry
6 organic eggs
5 ½ oz | 150 g sliced Emmental cheese
5 ½ oz | 150 g sliced pastrami
5 ½ oz | 150 g lamb's lettuce
3 tbsp olive oil
1 pinch of ground Espelette pepper (or hot Paprika)
1 pinch of *fleur de sel* (or other coarse sea salt)

Sauce Mornay (pour 120 g)

⅓ cup | 40 g all purpose flour
2 ¾ tbsp | 40 g unsalted butter
1 ½ oz | 40 g Parmesan cheese
1 ½ oz | 40 g Emmental cheese
½ cup | 125 ml heavy (double) cream
1 ⅔ cup | 400 ml whole milk
1 pinch of salt

1. Prepare the Mornay sauce: in a saucepan, melt the butter and stir in the flour over low heat. Add cream and milk and stir constantly until the mixture thickens. Add the grated Parmesan and Emmental. Salt and finish cooking. Place a plastic film over the sauce, making sure the entire surface is in contact with the film. Set aside.

2. Prepare the croque-madames: Unroll the puff pastry. Place the slices of pastrami over the entire surface of the pastry dough. Then, place the slices of Emmental cheese over the pastrami Finally, cover all the layers with a second layer of puff pastry dough. Dampen the edges of the puff pastry with water and press the edges together with your fingers to fully encase the filling.
Place in the Panini press and cook at 425°F |220°C for 3 minutes.

Equipment

Panini press or grilled sandwich maker

Piping bag fitted with a plain tip of ¼ inch | 6 mm

3. Wash the lamb's lettuce and pick out any bruised leaves. Fry an egg on a plancha or in a frying pan. You can use a pastry cutter for a neater presentation.

4. Cut the cooked croque-madame into rectangles measuring 4x1 inches | 11x3 cm. There should be 30 croque-madame soldiers in all. Place the egg in the middle of a plate with 5 soldiers around it.

5. Toss the lamb's lettuce with olive oil, a pinch of *fleur de sel* and the ground Espelette pepper. Arrange several florets between the soldiers. With the piping bag, garnish with 8 dots of Mornay cream. Continue with the 5 other servings.

Pairs well with
Our *Ceylan* tea

Cocktail Macarons

For 30 macarons of each flavor
Preparation: 30 minutes
Refrigeration time: 20–25 minutes

30 apricot macaron shells
See Basic Recipes for macarons, p. 300
Orange food dye

Carrot filling
12 oz | 345 g sand carrots (for the purée)
1 large carrot with greens
3 sheets of gelatin (¾ tbsp | 6 g powdered gelatin)
2 oranges
3 ¼ oz | 90 g young goat cheese
1 ⅔ tbsp | 30 ml white vinegar
1 tbsp of all-flower honey

Equipment
30 silicone Flexipan pomponettes molds, 1 ⅓ inch | 34 mm in diameter
Piping bag fitted with a plain tip, ⅖ inch | 10 mm in diameter
Mandoline slicer

Carrot macarons

1. Follow the Basic Recipe, p. 300 and add the orange food coloring.

2. Prepare the carrot purée. Soften gelatin in cold water. Squeeze to remove excess water. Process carrots, gelatin, zest and juice of 1 orange to a smooth purée. Pour the purée into the molds and place in refrigerator for 20 to 25 minutes.

3. With a mandoline, julienne the large carrot and save the greens for the garnish.

4. In a saucepan, bring the honey, juice of last orange and vinegar to a boil. Once the mixture has reduced, add the julienned carrots and bring back to a boil for 30 seconds. Pour into a clean bowl.

5. Place a hemisphere of carrot-orange purée in the middle of each macaron shell. With the piping bag, fitted with the tip, trace a crown of young goat cheese between the carrot purée and the macaron. Sprinkle a little of the julienne of caramelized carrot on the goat cheese. Garnish with a sprig of carrot green on the purée.

Parmesan macarons

1. Follow the Basic Recipe, p. 300 and add the red food coloring.

2. Prepare the parmesan cream: Soften the gelatin in cold water. Squeeze out the excess water.
Heat the cream and add the parmesan while stirring. Be careful not to scorch the cream. Add the softened gelatin. Blend until smooth and pour the mixture into the hemispherical molds. Place in refrigerator for 20–25 minutes.

3. Place a hemisphere of parmesan cream in the middle of each macaron shell. With the piping bag, fitted with the tip, trace a crown of cream cheese between the sphere and the macaron. Grate some Parmesan over the cream cheese. Garnish with a grind of red pepper over each hemisphere.

30 rose macaron shells
See Basic Recipes for macarons, p. 300
Red food coloring

Parmesan cream
1 ¼ cup | 245 ml cream
70 g grated parmesan + 15 g for the garnish
3 sheets of gelatin (¾ tbsp | 6 g powdered gelatin)
6 Tbsp | 90 g cream cheese
Pondicherry red pepper

Equipment
30 silicone Flexipan pomponettes molds, 1 ⅓ inch | 34 mm in diameter
Piping bag fitted with a plain tip, ⅜ 8 inch | 10 mm in diameter

Maceration time: 1 hour
Cooking time: 20 minutes

30 pistachio macaron shells
See Basic Recipes for macarons, p. 300
Green food coloring

Foie gras filling
4 oz | 120 g fig chutney (see below)
6 oz | 180 g foie gras
1 ½ tsp | 3 g pistachios
1 punnet of green shiso microgreens

Fig chutney (4 ¼ oz | 120 g)
1 oz | 30 g fresh figs
1 oz | 30 g soft, dried figs
½ tbsp | 10 ml white vinegar
¾ tbsp | 15 ml white, balsamic vinegar
2 ½ tsp | 10 g granulated sugar
½ tbsp | 10 g all-flower honey
½ tbsp | 10 ml of freshly squeezed lemon juice
1 cinnamon stick
1 pinch of ground pepper

Equipment
Pastry cutter, 1 inch | 3 cm in diameter
Microplane grater
Piping bag fitted with a plain tip,
²/₅ inch | 10 mm in diameter

Foie gras macarons

1. Follow the Basic Recipe, p. 300 and add the green food coloring.

2. Prepare the fig chutney: dice the fresh and dried figs finely. Mix together with sugar and lemon juice and allow to macerate for 1 hour.

3. After 1 hour, pour the white vinegar and honey into a saucepan. Bring to a simmer and allow to reduce by half. Add the fig mixture, balsamic vinegar and spices. Bring to a boil and allow to cook for 20 minutes. Allow to cool and place in the refrigerator. Remove the cinnamon stick and process the chutney.

4. Slice the foie gras into 1 inch | 3 cm slivers and with the pastry cutter, cut out disks, 1 inch | 3 cm in diameter.

5. Place a disk of foie gras in the middle of each macaron shell. With the piping bag, fitted with the tip, trace a crown of chutney between the foie gras and the macaron. With the Microplane, grate a little pistachio over the foie gras and garnish with a sprig of shiso microgreens.

Salmon macarons

30 lemon macaron shells
See Basic Recipes for macarons, p. 300
Yellow food coloring

Salmon filling
4 oz | 120 g smoked salmon, fillet
½ cup | 110 g cream cheese
½ lime

Equipment
30 silicone Flexipan pomponettes molds, 1 ⅓-inch | 34-mm in diameter
Piping bag fitted with a plain tip, ⅖ inch | 10 mm in diameter

1. Follow the Basic Recipe, p. 300 and add the yellow food coloring.

2. Cream the cream cheese with the lime juice and most of the zest (save some for the garnish). Cut the smoked salmon filet into ½ inch | 1 ½ cm cubes.

3. Arrange 4 salmon cubes in a pyramid in the middle of the macaron. With the piping bag fitted with its tip, pipe 3 large dots of cream cheese around the pyramid, covering as much of the macaron as possible. Garnish with a sprinkle of lime zest.

Pairs well with
Our *Darjeeling* tea

Cat's Tongues

Makes 50 biscuits
Preparation: 20 minutes
Cooking time: 10–12 minutes

9 tbsp | 125 g butter
1 ⅓ cups | 160 g confectioners' (icing) sugar
1 packet of vanilla sugar (or 2 tsp sugar + 1 tsp vanilla extract)
2 organic egg whites
1 ¼ cups | 160 g cake (SR) flour

Equipment
Piping bag fitted with a ⅕ inch | 5 mm plain tip

1. Cut the butter in small pieces and put in a heatproof bowl set over a pan of gently simmering water. Using a wooden spoon, work the butter until soft and creamy. Remove from heat and whisk until smooth.
Add each of the following ingredients one by one, making sure to mix well after each addition: confectioners' sugar, vanilla sugar and the egg whites. Whisk together.

2. Sift the flour and stir into the mixture with a wooden spoon until the batter is homogeneous.

3. Preheat the oven to 325°F | 165°C | gas mark 3. Transfer the batter to the piping bag fitted with a plain tip. Pipe 2 ⅓ inch | 6 cm long strips onto a baking sheet lined with parchment paper.
Leave space between each biscuit as they spread during baking.

Pairs well with
Our *Chéri* tea

4. Place sheet in oven and bake for 10-12 minutes until golden.
Allow the biscuits to cool to room temperature on the baking sheet before removing with a spatula. When they have cooled completely, store in an airtight container.

You can dip the biscuits in dark, milk or white chocolate or white chocolate colored with fat soluble food coloring (pink) and leave them to dry on a piece of parchment paper

Chef's tip

Plain biscuits are delicious with a chocolate mousse or a fruit salad.

THE RIGHT DOSE

A good cup of tea is a precise art and requires just the right quantity of leaves according to the size of the teapot or teacup.

NEVER TOO MUCH
Although there is no hard and fast rule governing dosage, there are several important principles. Professionals advise 2 g, i.e. a small teaspoon, for a 100–150 ml cup. This can then be adapted for the number of cups desired or the volume of the teapot. Another simple English rule advises "one teaspoon per person and one for the pot".
The perfect cup however is a very personal matter. Some like it strong, others weak. Some with milk and sugar, others pale and gentle. Some prefer a short infusion with a large dose of tea for a strong yet aromatic touch. Others like to stew their brew.

IT DEPENDS ON THE TEA
Doses vary according to the type of tea. Black tea generally demands smaller doses than green and white teas. As a general guide: white tea, 2 teaspoons per cup; green tea, 1–2 teaspoons per cup and 2–3 teaspoons for a Sencha; Oolong, ½ teaspoon; black tea, 1–2 heaped teaspoons. The aim is to obtain a gentle yet flavorsome and aromatic drink.

All Chocolate Tartlets

Makes 8 tartlets
Preparation: 1 ¾ hours
Cooking time: 30 minutes
Resting time: 1 ½ hours

Sweet cocoa pastry
9 oz | 250 g sweet almond pastry dough, see p. 297
2 ¾ tbsp | 20 g unsweetened cocoa powder (to full 16 oz | 450 g pastry dough recipe)

Flourless chocolate biscuit
1 ⅗ oz | 45 g chocolate, 60 to 70 % cocoa powder
3 organic eggs
5 ½ tbsp | 65 g granulated sugar

Chocolate ganache
10 ½ oz | 300 g chocolate, 65 to 75 % cocoa powder
1 ⅓ cups | 300 ml single cream
7 tbsp | 100 g butter, room temperature
1 bar of chocolate (7 oz | 200 g)
Unsweetened cocoa for garnish

SWEET PASTRY DOUGH

1. Prepare the sweet almond pastry dough as explained on p. 297. Sift the cocoa powder with the flour.

2. Butter tartlet molds.
On a floured work surface, roll out the dough to ⅒ inch | 2 mm thick. With a pastry cutter, cut out circles roughly 4 ½ 5 inches | 12 cm in diameter. Press into molds. Allow to rest in refrigerator for 1 hour.

Preheat the oven to 325°F | 165°F | gas mark 3. Meanwhile, using a fork, prick the dough to avoid bubbles during baking. Cover dough with parchment paper, carefully pressing into the corners and working up the sides to keep the dough in place during baking. Place dried beans on top of the paper. Place the molds in the oven and bake for 15 to 20 minutes. Remove the tartlet shells from the oven. Remove the dried beans and parchment paper and allow the shells to cool.

Equipment

8 tartlet molds, 3 inch | 8 cm diameter and ⅘ inch | 2 cm high
Piping bag fitted with a ¼ inch | 7–8 mm plain tip

FLOURLESS CHOCOLATE BISCUITS

3. Break the chocolate into pieces and place in a heatproof bowl. Place over gently simmering water and wait for the chocolate to melt. Remove when it is warm but not hot.
Separate the egg whites from the yolks. Place the yolks in a large bowl with 3 tbsp | 35 g of sugar and beat until foamy.
Whisk the egg whites in a smaller bowl until they form soft peaks. Add 2 ½ tbsp of sugar and continue to whisk until they form stiff peaks.
Pour ¼ of the whisked egg whites into the yolk and sugar mixture. Stir in the melted chocolate. Finally, gently fold in the rest of the egg whites.

4. Preheat the oven to 325°F | 165°F | gas mark 3. Line a baking sheet with parchment paper. Fill the piping bag with biscuit batter. Pipe, spiraling outward, disks that are ¾ inch | 2 cm less in diameter than the tartlets. Place the pan in the oven and bake for approximately 10 minutes. The biscuit should be slightly dry. Remove from oven and allow to cool.

CHOCOLATE GANACHE

5. Chop the chocolate finely and place in a large bowl. In a saucepan, bring the cream to a boil. Pour half the boiling cream onto the chocolate and whisk in circles to emulsify the chocolate and cream mixture. Add the rest of the boiled cream and continue whisking in the same manner.

6. Dice the butter into small cubes and stir into the ganache with a rubber spatula until smooth. Immediately assemble the tartlets.

ASSEMBLY
7. Pour a thin layer of ganache ($1/10$ inch | 2–3 mm) into the bottom of the sweet pastry shells. Place the chocolate biscuit, press lightly. Fill to the edge with the rest of the ganache.
Allow to harden at room temperature for 30 minutes.

8. Decorate the top of the tartlets. With a vegetable peeler or a paring knife, shave off curls of chocolate from the chocolate bar directly onto the tartlets. Avoid having to touch them. Dust lightly with unsweetened cocoa.

Pairs well with
Our *Vénus* tea

Rose Cream Puffs

Makes 25 to 30 cream puffs
Preparation: 1 hour and 15 minutes
+ Basic Recipes
Cooking time: 40 minutes

Cream puffs
Cream puff dough: see Basic Recipes, p. 299
1 ½ tbsp | 20 g butter for baking sheet

Rose pastry cream
3 cups | 400 g pastry cream: see Basic Recipe, p. 302
1 tbsp rose water
2 tbsp rose syrup
3 drops natural rose essential oil

Rose fondant
3 oz | 80 g white chocolate
4 oz | 120 g white pouring fondant
5 tbsp rose syrup
4 drops natural rose essential oil
a few drops of red food coloring

PASTRY CREAM

1. Prepare the pastry cream (see Basic Recipe, p. 302) and keep in the refrigerator.

CREAM PUFFS

2. Prepare the cream puff dough (see Basic Recipe, p. 299).
Preheat the oven to 350°F | 180° C | gas mark 4. Transfer the dough to the piping bag fitted with the ½ inch | 10 mm plain tip. Pipe 1 ½ inch | 4 cm diameter dough onto a buttered baking sheet.

3. Place in oven and bake. After 8 to 10 minutes, when they will have started to puff up, open the oven door very slightly, about ⅛ inch | 2–3 mm, to allow the steam to escape. Bake the cream puffs for approximately 30 minutes with the oven door slightly ajar, until golden. Remove from the oven and allow to cool on a wire rack.

Garnish
25–30 raspberries

Equipment
Piping bag fitted with a ½ inch | 10 mm plain tip
Piping bag fitted with a ⅓ inch | 8 mm plain tip

ROSE PASTRY CREAM
4. Remove pastry cream from the refrigerator. Whisk until smooth, eliminating any lumps, and add the rose water, syrup and essential oil.

FILLING
5. Using the ⅓ inch | 8 mm plain tip without the piping bag, poke a hole in the bottom of each cream puff.
Transfer the rose pastry cream to the piping bag fitted with the ⅓ inch | 8 mm plaint tip.
Fill the cooled cream puffs by piping rose cream into the holes.

ROSE FONDANT
6. Melt the white chocolate in a heatproof bowl set over a pan of gently simmering water or in the microwave at medium power. In a saucepan, slightly warm the pouring fondant with the syrup and essential oil, and add the melted white chocolate. Add a few drops of food coloring to obtain the desired color. Stir until smooth.
Dip the tops of the cream puffs into this preparation to glaze and decorate with a raspberry. Allow to set and keep in the refrigerator.

Pairs well with
Our *Mistinguette* tea

LET IT BREW

If you steep tea for too long, the bitterness of the leaf will disguise the true aroma. Like all good relationships, tea needs time and space.

GIVE IT TIME
The ideal brew requires the right brewing time, just as each tea type requires the right dose and water temperature. Some teas require barely a minute, others much longer. Brewing time is crucial to obtain the perfect balance of tannins, theine and aromatics. Steeping for too long disturbs this balance. Stewed tea contains too much tannin and is bitter, acrid and unpleasant. Patience is a virtue but too much can be a bad thing.

GIVE IT SPACE
For tea to infuse properly, it needs space for the leaf to swell and open. Leaf size influences brewing time. The smaller the leaf, the shorter it should steep. Broken leaves need only two minutes. Tea ball strainers restrict the leaf's contact with the water and so, imprison the aroma. As you'll have noticed after serving, tea leaves take up more room in the pot than they did on the spoon, so bigger pots are required for bigger doses.

TEA Party

Tea Party

Tea is the drink of pioneers in the United States. It's a brew drunk on-the-go, served from a Thermos in the Cadillac or out of a cardboard mug. It represents their conquering spirit, and flies in the face of convention.

TEA AND ETIQUETTE

One delightful moment at the heart of David Fincher's movie, *The Curious Case of Benjamin Button* (2008), illustrates the difference between English and American tea. One night in an abandoned hotel in Russia, the movie's American protagonist Benjamin Button trudges downstairs and makes tea for the distinctly English Elizabeth Abbott, with whom he has fallen in love. Rather than swoon at the gesture, Elizabeth is taken aback by his laissez-faire approach to the beverage and his lack of tea decorum. "It's better to let it steep a little," she admonishes him, "There is a proper way to make tea." "From where I'm from," replies Benjamin, "people just want it to be hot."

Traditionally, Americans are coffee drinkers and when they do drink tea, unlike Benjamin, they generally prefer it iced. Canada meanwhile consumes nearly four times more tea than its southern neighbor. In the United States, there is a great difference in scale and points of reference with Europe and Asia. Drinks are served in large portions, mugs and tall glasses and served to be drunk on-the-go. In a coffee shop, after placing your order, you'll be

asked: "To stay or to go?" – it is never taken for granted that you want to sit down. Tea is drunk everywhere, on the road, in the street, at work, wherever, whenever, throughout the day. Freedom rules. And the latest research into tea and its beneficial medical effects is winning over new aficionados among the health-conscious.

If there is one aspect of tea that the American people never forget it is the role tea has played in American history and the importance of the Boston Tea Party. In the US, tea is a symbol of liberty.

REBEL WITHOUT A TEACUP

Tea was imported into the New World by the Dutch in the 17th century. Its consumption became more widespread in the course of the following century. In the late 18th century, it was appreciated by a third of the colonial population and was a leading import. In 1773, the British Parliament voted in the Tea Act to boost the ailing British East India Company and undercut the price of illegal tea. The Act allowed the company to reduce its massive stocks by exporting them to America duty-free; colonial taxes paid to the British government, however, remained in place. The decision incensed colonists and turned them against the English government. On 16 December 1773, Boston radicals disguised as Indian Mohawks boarded an East India Company ship and emptied the cargo into the port of Boston, turning the harbor into a giant teapot. This storm in a tea ship gradually turned into the American War of Independence. The rebellion was emulated in the other thirteen British colonies and even high-society ladies boycotted the beverage, a habit that was restored after the declaration of independence, 4th July 1776.

TEA DEVELOPMENT

America is responsible for two pioneering innovations in tea that have aided its industrial development: iced tea and tea bags. In the sweltering heat of the Saint Louis World's Fair in 1904, the tea trader Richard Blechynden decided that a cool drink would be more profitable than a hot one. Iced tea was already a household staple in the southern states, but Blechynden's intervention sealed recognition nationwide. 1903 had seen the first tea bag patents, and the idea met with commercial success in 1908, when the New York-based importer, Thomas Sullivan, decided to package tea leaves in silk tea bags to reduce delivery costs. Clients were instructed to remove the tea from the pouches, but many simply dunked them in their pot, as the porous bags proved very practical for brewing their favorite drink. Sullivan went onto improve his "invention" by replacing silk with cotton muslin and from the 1920s tea bag production became industrialized. In 1930, William Hermanson patented the heat-sealed paper fiber tea bag. A year previously in Germany, Adolf Rambold perfected the same style of sachet. Although successful, the enterprise had one important downside: tea was now ground into dust so, while manufacture and packaging became easier, the quality of tea suffered. The 1980s saw the return of muslin tea bags, offering simplicity and quality.

Bagels and Salmon

Serves 6 people
Preparation: 20 minutes

6 plain mini-bagels nature, 2 inches | 6 cm in diameter
8 ½ oz | 240 g sliced smoked salmon
²/₅ cup | 100 g cream cheese
1 oz | 30 g salmon roe
1 cucumber
10 sprigs of chives
1 punnet of coriander microgreens
Juice and zest of 1 lime
Ground Espelette pepper (or hot Paprika)
Fleur de sel (or other coarse sea salt)

Equipment
Mandoline
Pastry cutter, 2 inch | 6 cm in diameter
Small offset spatula

1. Prepare the garnish: wash and mince the chives. Mix the cream cheese, chives and lime juice. Wash the cucumber and slice it thinly with a mandoline. With the pastry cutter, cut out circles of cucumber the same size as the bagels. Repeat with the slices of smoked salmon.

2. Assemble the bagels: cut each bagel in half horizontally. With the offset spatula, spread both halves with a generous amount of the cream cheese and chive mixture. On the bottom half of the bagel, place in the following order: cucumber, salmon and a second slice of cucumber. Cover with the top half of the bagel.

• • •

3. Cut each bagel sandwich in two. Place the bagels cut side up on a plate. Garnish with the salmon roe, a sprinkle of coriander microgreens, shreds of lime zest, a pinch of Espelette pepper and a pinch of *fleur de sel*.

Pairs well with
Our *Ceylan* tea

GET-UP-AND-GO

Tea is a marvelous stimulant, but what makes it such a great pick-me-up? Theine or caffeine?.

THEINE AND CAFFEINE?
Theine is actually the same molecule as caffeine. Tea-leaves contain 2.5–5 %, with higher concentrations in the buds than in the lower leaves. Theine is very soluble and 80% of its content in leaves floods out within the first minute of brewing. Theine stimulates the nervous system and promotes mental awareness without over-exciting the brain as its absorption into the bloodstream takes longer and is more uniform than coffee. There is less caffeine in a cup of tea than in an espresso (200 mg per liter vs. 1,900 mg per liter).

SETTING A FEW TEA MATTERS STRAIGHT
A quick brew does not limit the effect of theine. It is the tannins and amino acids liberated later that ease its absorption by the digestive system. The theine in tea can be reduced by discarding the first brief infusion, but this also discards valuable aromas.
It is thought that dark robust teas contain more theine than lighter teas. This however is not always the case: China's prestigious White Hair Silver Needle white tea, for example, contains more theine than a Ceylon Orange Pekoe.

Lobster Rolls

Serves 6 people
Preparation: 40 minutes
Cooking time: 8 minutes

2 Canadian lobsters
12 plain brioche buns
1 butterhead lettuce
1 lime (Juice and zest of)
1 bunch of chives
1 pinch of ground Espelette pepper (or hot Paprika)
1 pinch of *fleur de sel* (or other coarse sea salt)

Mayonnaise (6oz | 165 g)
1 organic egg yolk
1 tbsp | 17 g Dijon mustard
½ cup | 130 ml vegetable oil
3 ⅓ tsp | 20 ml white vinegar
1 pinch of ground Espelette pepper (or hot Paprika)
1 pinch of table salt

1. Separate the claws from the body of the lobsters. Plunge all the pieces into a court-bouillon, flavored with your favorite herbs and spices. Allow the body to cook for 5 minutes and the claws for 8 minutes. Immediately refresh in a large volume of ice and water. Carefully remove all the meat from the bodies, claws and elbows of the lobsters. Set aside on paper towels.

2. Prepare the mayonnaise: Place the yolk in a bowl with rounded edges and just big enough to hold the desired quantity of mayonnaise. Add the mustard, salt and Espelette pepper. Whisk until all the ingredients are fully incorporated. Slowly pour a slow stream of oil while continuing to whisk briskly. Add the vinegar and season to taste. Place in the refrigerator.

3. Cut the lobster meat into ⅓ inch | 1 cm cubes. Mince the chives and stir most of them into the mayonnaise (saving some for the garnish).

•••

Adjust seasoning by adding the lime juice and zest to taste. Toss the lobster cubes with half the mayonnaise.

4. Wash and dry the butterhead lettuce. Trim the leaves to fit the buns (with a preference for the outside leaves). Mince the rest of the leaves and add them to the other half of the chive-mayonnaise sauce.

5. Trim the top and bottom of each bun for easier browning. Slice the buns in half, stopping ¾ of the way through. The buns should open but not separate. Toast both sides of the bun in a dry pan. Do the same for the other buns.

6. Fill the buns, starting with the lettuce-chive mayonnaise towards the back of the bun. Pile a generous amount of the lobster-mayonnaise mixture on top. Slip a trimmed leaf of lettuce between the lobster filling and the bun. It should hang slightly over the edge and will stay in place thanks to the filling.

7. Place 2 lobster rolls at an angle on a plate with a dab of mayonnaise under each to prevent them from sliding. Season with the *fleur de sel* and the Espelette pepper. Garnish with the remaining chives.

Pairs well with
Our *Earl Grey* tea

Mini-hamburgers

Serves 6 people
Preparation: 40 minutes
Cooking time (hamburgers): 5–10 minutes
Cooking time (tomatoes): 4 hours

10 ½ oz | 300 g ground (minced) beef
12 mini brioche buns
⅓ cup | 100 g honey mustard
½ bunch tarragon
2 ½ oz | 70 g sliced Gruyère cheese
2 heads of butterhead lettuce
¾ tsp | 50 ml olive oil (for frying)
1 pinch of ground Espelette pepper (or hot Paprika)
1 pinch of *fleur de sel* (or other coarse sea salt)

Semi-dried tomatoes (2 ½ oz | 70 g)
3 tomatoes
½ tsp | 2 ml olive oil
1 ½ g granulated sugar (optional)
1 sprig of thyme
1 pinch of table salt

Equipment
Pastry cutter the same size as the brioche buns

1. Prepare the semi-dried tomatoes: preheat the oven to 195°F | 90°C | gas mark ¼. Peel and seed the tomatoes. Cut each into four wedges. Place in a bowl and carefully toss them with the olive oil and salt. (You can add sugar if you wish). Line a baking sheet with parchment paper. Spread the tomato wedges over the baking sheet, making sure to leave ample room between each. Sprinkle the thyme over the tomatoes and place in the oven for 4 hours. Check on them regularly and oil them lightly if needed. Turn over those tomatoes whose tops are too dry or whose bottoms are too wet. Remove each when they are fully dried and allow to cool.

2. Prepare the green sauce: blend the honey mustard with the tarragon leaves.

3. With the pastry cutter, cut disks out of the sliced Gruyère cheese. Trim the outside lettuce leaves to the size of the hamburger buns.

•••

4. Trim the bottom edge of the brioche bun in order to toast it. Slice each bun through the middle, taking care to not cut it all the way through. The bun should open but not separate. Toast the cut edge on a plancha or in a dry frying pan. Repeat for the other buns.

5. Shape 12 mini-hamburgers, weighing ⅘ oz | 25 g each. Preheat the oven to 350°F | 180°C | gas mark 4. Grill one side of the patties on a plancha or fry them in a frying pan according to your preference. Flip them over and season with a pinch of salt and a pinch of ground Espelette pepper. Place a circle of Gruyère cheese on each. Finish cooking them in the oven. Total cooking time is between 5 and 10 minutes.

6. Spread both sides of the inside of the bun with the green sauce. Place a leaf of lettuce, a dried tomato and finally the mini-patty with Gruyère. Arrange two mini-hamburgers on each plate.

Pairs well with
Our *Senchayamato* tea

ICED TEA

An American invention that has the charm of the American way of life and offers a refreshing healthy alternative to sodas.

BOSTON HARBOR IN A GLASS

There is nothing more refreshing than a long drink of iced tea in the dog days of summer. Iced tea is not made by cooling hot tea, but by steeping tea leaves in water at room temperature for several hours: one hour for green tea, three hours for black tea or Oolong. After the leaves are removed the tea is refrigerated and sugar or crushed ice may be added when serving. Slices of orange can be added to orange blossom Oolong; redcurrants or red fruit to blackberry, violet or rose teas; and slices of apple to a vanilla tea. To create a delicious, fresh, detox drink, infuse grated ginger and organic lemon peel in iced green tea.

COLD WATER INFUSION

Tea bars are spreading across Europe where many purveyors are using the cold-water brew technique to achieve delicate tannins and subtle aromas. Depending on the tea variety, the leaves are infused for anywhere between 30 minutes and 8 hours.

Cheesecake

17 ½ oz | 500 g cream cheese
1 cup | 200 g granulated sugar
½ cup + 5 ½ tbsp | 200 ml heavy (double) cream
2 ⅓ tbsp | 7 ml full-fat milk
2 organic eggs
2 organic egg yolks
½ vanilla pod (seeds from)
The grated zest of 1 lemon

Crust
2 cups | 250 g flour
⅔ cup | 150 g butter
1 oz | 30 g ground almonds (almond flour)
⅔ cup | 90 g confectioners' (icing) sugar
1 pinch of salt

Equipment
Springform cake mold, 9 inch | 22 cm diameter and 2 inch | 4 ½ cm high

Pairs well with
Our *Earl Grey Rose* tea

Serves 8 people
Preparation: 1 ¼ hours
Cooking time: 1 ½ hours
Resting time: 1 hour
Refrigerate: 12 hours

1. For the crust: mix all the ingredients with your hands (or the pastry hook of your stand mixer). When the dough starts to come together, transfer to clean bowl and refrigerate for 1 hour.

2. Preheat the oven to 300°F | 150°C | gas mark 2. Roll out the crust to a uniform thickness of ⅕ inch | 5 mm and place at the bottom of the mold. Place in oven and bake for 30 minutes. The crust should be lightly golden.

3. Beat together the cream cheese, sugar, zest and vanilla seeds. Slowly add the eggs and egg yolks, and finally the cream and milk.

4. Pour the batter onto the baked crust and bake at 240°F | 115°C | gas mark ½ for approximately 1 hour. The edges should be firm while the center should tremble slightly. Refrigerate the cheesecake overnight before removing from pan.

Bugnes

Makes 20 bugnes
Preparation: 30 minutes
Cooking time: 2–3 minutes
Resting time: 1 hour

1 lemon, unwaxed
2 tbsp | 25 g granulated sugar
2 pinches of *fleur de sel* (or other coarse sea salt)
1 tbsp orange blossom water
2 organic eggs
5 tbsp | 75 g butter
2 cups | 250 g cake (SR) flour + 2 ½ tbsp | 20 g for work surface
2 ½ tbsp | 20 g confectioners' (icing) sugar

Equipment
Fryer
Fluted wheel (optional)

1. Zest the lemon and toss with the sugar in a small bowl.
In another bowl, dissolve the salt and orange blossom water.
Set aside.
Remove the eggs from the refrigerator and bring to room temperature.

2. Soften the butter in a large, heatproof bowl set over a pan of gently simmering water or in the microwave until it resembles cream cheese.
Be careful not to let it melt.
Add the sugar and zest to the butter and whisk until creamy.
Add the room temperature eggs one at a time, then the salt and orange blossom water.
Add the flour and mix just enough to incorporate all the flour.
Allow dough to rest for 1 hour.

•••

3. Divide the dough into 2 or 3 (smaller portions will be easier to roll out).
On a floured surface, roll out the dough to a thickness of 1 mm.
Using a fluted wheel or a knife, cut the dough into diamonds, 4 inches | 10 cm long and 1 ½–2 inch | 4–5 cm wide.
In the center of each diamond, make a small slit lengthwise approximately 1 ¼ inch | 3 cm long.

4. Preheat the fryer to 325°F–340°F | 160°C–170°C.
Fry each bugne for 2 minutes in hot oil, turning them over once while cooking.
Drain on a paper towel until completely cooled.
Dust with confectioners' sugar.

Pairs well with
Our *Caramel* tea

"WATER IS THE MOTHER OF TEA"

This Chinese proverb highlights the important role of water in preparing tea. The tea leaves can only release their aroma, color and flavor in contact with water.

THE RIGHT WATER ...
Depending on the water you choose, you won't obtain the same brew. Calcium and chlorine are incompatible with good tea. The water used should have a neutral pH and low mineral content, so even tap water with low levels of chlorine and chalk is fine. Water filter pitchers help soften water. You can also use spring water.

... AT THE RIGHT TEMPERATURE
The water you use shouldn't boil. When water reaches boiling point, gas evaporates, including the oxygen contained in the water. Oxygen helps aroma molecules achieve their gaseous state and thus helps the perception of flavor in the process of retronasal olfaction. This process combines both our senses of taste and smell – not direct smell but the aroma molecules that are shunted up our nose as we chew and swallow.
Each type of tea has an ideal brewing temperature. Green teas vary between 50°C (122°F) and 70°C (158°F), black teas between 85°C (185°F) and 98 °C (208°F). Some fragrant teas release their aromas at 70°C (158°F), others at 90°C (194°F). Use an electric kettle that heats tea to the required temperature. The ideal tasting temperature is between 40°C (104°F) and 50°C (122°F), which leaves you a few precious minutes to prepare your own tea ritual.

Doughnuts (Beignets)

Makes 20 doughnuts
Preparation: 1 hour
Cooking time: 3–4 minutes
Resting time: 4 hours

Batter
1 ¾ cups +2 tbsp | 235 g cake (SR) flour + 2 ½ tbsp | 20 g
⅓ cup | 65 g granulated sugar
2 oz | 60 g fresh yeast
2 tsp | 10 g salt
5 organic egg yolks
3 ⅓ tbsp | 50 ml whole milk
4 ½ tbsp | 65 g butter

Pre-ferment
2 cups + 2 tbsp | 265 g cake (SR) flour
⅙ oz | 5 g fresh yeast

Finishing sugar
¼ cup | 50 g granulated sugar
⅛ tsp | 2 pinches of powdered cinnamon

PRE-FERMENT

1. Place the flour in a large bowl. Dilute the fresh yeast in ¾ cup (minus) 1tsp | 170 ml of lukewarm water and pour over the flour. Mix well.
Allow to double in volume at room temperature for approximately 1 hour.

DOUGHNUT BATTER

2. Place the flour and sugar in a large bowl.
Add the yeast and salt on separate sides of the flour. Do not allow them to touch before you are ready to mix.
Add egg yolks and milk. Mix just enough to incorporate all ingredients and for the dough to come away from the sides of the bowl. Add softened butter. Incorporate the pre-ferment. Mix until dough is smooth.
Allow the dough to double in volume for 1 hour. Punch it down and roll the dough into a ball before placing it in the refrigerator for 30 minutes.

...

•••

DOUGHNUTS (BEIGNETS)

3. Once the dough has chilled, divide into 2 oz | 50 g portions and fold each over onto itself to form smooth balls. Place each on a clean, floured dishcloth in a warm spot (77°F–86°F | 25°C–30°C) until double in size (approximately 1 ½ hours).

4. Preheat the deep fryer to 325°F–340°F | 160°C –170°C. Carefully lower each ball into the hot oil. Fry each side 3 to 4 minutes until golden brown. With a skimmer, remove each doughnut and drain on paper towels.

5. Allow to cool while you mix the sugar and cinnamon. Roll each doughnut (beignet) in the mixture to coat.

Pairs well with
Our *Caramel* tea

Basic Recipes

Shortcrust pastry

Makes 1 shell for a tart for 8 people
Preparation: 20 minutes
Refrigeration: 1 hour

2 cups | 200 g cake (SR) flour
7 tbs | 100 g butter
1 ½ organic egg yolks
2 ⅓ tbs | 35 ml water or milk
¾ tsp | 4 g of salt
2 organic egg yolks

Makes 30 tartlets, 1 ⅓ inch | 3 ½ cm diameter
Preparation: 30 minutes
Refrigeration: 1 hour
Cooking time: 15–20 minutes

1 ½ cups | 150 g cake flour
⅓ cup | 75 g unsalted butter, room temperature +
1 ½ tbsp | 20 g for the molds
1 organic egg yolk
1 ¾ | 25 ml cold water or milk
½ tsp | 3 g salt

1. Dissolve the salt in cold water (or milk).

2. In a large bowl, work the butter until creamy (ideally, the butter should be taken out of the refrigerator at least 30 minutes before. You can also heat it in a microwave for 30 seconds on the lowest setting). Add the egg yolk and cream the mixture. Add the flour and work it in with the tips of your fingers until the dough resembles coarse sand. Quickly add the water (or milk) and form the dough into a ball. Wrap tightly with plastic wrap and refrigerate for at least 1 hour before using.

SHORTCRUST PASTRY FOR TARTLETS

3. Remove the dough from the refrigerator and allow it to rest for approximately 15 minutes.

4. Preheat the oven to 350°F | 180°C | gas mark 4. On a lightly floured work surface, roll the dough out to a uniform thickness of ¹⁄₁₂ inch | 2 mm. With the pastry cutter, cut out 30 disks with a diameter of 1 ⅓ inch | 4 cm.

5. Butter the molds. Place the disks in the molds and press with your fingers to fully adhere the dough to the bottom of the molds. Cover the bottom of the shells with dried beans to maintain the shells' shape while baking. Lower oven to 325°F | 165°F | gas mark 3 and bake for 15–20 minutes.

Makes 16 oz | 450 g of dough
Preparation: 20 minutes
Resting time: minimum of 2 hours, preferably 12 hours

½ cup | 120 g very cold butter
½ cup + 1 tbsp | 70 g confectioners' (icing) sugar
¼ cup | 25 g ground almonds (almond flour)
1 pinch of *fleur de sel* (or other coarse sea salt)
1 pinch of vanilla powder or a few drops of vanilla extract (optional)
1 organic egg
1 ⅔ cups | 200 g cake (SR) flour

Chef's tip

This recipe makes 16 oz | 450 g of dough. The final texture depends entirely on the proportions for 1 egg. Therefore, I suggest you make the entire recipe even if you do not need that much dough.

6. Remove tartlet shells from the oven and wait until they have cooled before removing the dried beans. You can now fill the shells with the filling of your choice. Then can be stored in an airtight container in a dry place for a week.

Sweet Almond Pastry

1. Dice butter into small pieces in a bowl. Work the butter into a smooth mass. Add the following ingredients one at a time, making sure to fully incorporate them before adding the next: sifted confectioners' sugar, ground almonds, *fleur de sel*, vanilla, egg and flour. Mix only enough to bring the dough together; do not overwork the dough. This will give the pastry its desired crumbly texture.

2. Form the dough into a ball and cover in plastic wrap. Refrigerate for at least 2 hours before using. If possible, it is preferable to prepare the dough the night before. It will be easier to roll out. The dough will keep for up to 5 days in the refrigerator.

Basic Recipes

Makes 2 lbs | 1 kg
Preparation: 30 minutes
Resting time: 9 hours

2 ½ tsp | 10 g de *fleur de sel*
(or other coarse sea salt)
5 tbsp | 75 g butter +
1 ½ cups + 4 tbsp | 400 g very cold butter
4 cups | 500 g cake (SR) flour

Puff pastry

1. Dissolve the *fleur de sel* in 1 cup | 250 ml of room temperature water.
In a small saucepan, melt the 5 tbsp | 75 g of butter over low heat.
Place the flour in a large bowl, add the salt-water mixture, then the melted butter. Mix together with your fingertips until the dough is homogenous.
Do not overwork the dough.

2. Gather the dough (known as the *détrempe*), place on a clean work surface and shape into a 6x6-inch | 15x15-cm square. Wrap in plastic wrap and refrigerate for 1 hour until firm.

3. Put the 1 ½ cups + 4 tbsp | 400 g of chilled butter on a sheet of parchment paper. With a rolling pin, pound the butter to soften it. Using the parchment paper, fold the butter back on itself and continue to soften it. It should have the same consistency as the dough. Form the butter into a 6x6-inch | 15x15-cm square. Roll out the *détrempe* to obtain a 12x12 inch | 30x30 cm square and place the butter in the center on a diagonal. Fold the 4 corners of the dough into the center to completely enclose the butter.

4. Once the package is complete, roll out the square into a rectangle 24 inches | 60 cm long, then fold it in thirds (like a business letter). Give this folded dough (called the *pâton*) a quarter turn, roll it out again to length of 24 inch | 60 cm and once again, fold it into thirds. Each time you fold the dough into thirds, you have completed a single turn. You should turn the dough a total of 6 times, allowing the dough to rest for 2 hours in the refrigerator after every 2 turns.

5. Once you have completed the 6 turns, allow the dough to rest in the refrigerator for at least 2 hours, ideally overnight. Keep in the refrigerator until ready to use.

Cream Puff (Choux) Dough

1. Sift the flour. In a saucepan, bring milk, ½ cup (minus) 1tbsp | 100 ml water, sugar, salt and butter to a boil. Remove from heat. Incorporate the sifted flour into the hot liquid, mixing energetically with a spatula until homogenous.
Return the saucepan to low heat and continue stirring vigorously for 1 minute to "dry out" the dough mix.

2. Transfer dough to a bowl. Add eggs one at a time, carefully incorporating each with a spatula before adding the next. Keep mixing until dough is homogenous. It is now ready to be used.

Makes 25 small cream puffs
Preparation: 20 minutes
Cooking time: 3 minutes

1 cup + ½ tbsp | 120 g cake flour
½ cup (minus) 1tbsp | 100 ml whole milk
1 tbsp | 10 g granulated sugar
1 pinch of salt
5 ½ tbsp | 80 g butter
4 organic eggs

Basic Recipes

Makes approximately 50 macarons
Preparation: 50 minutes
Cooking time: 14 minutes

3 cups + 3 ⅔ tbsp | 275 g ground almonds (almond flour)
2 cups + 1 tbsp | 250 g confectioners' (icing) sugar
6 organic egg whites + ½ organic egg white
1 cup + 1 tbsp | 210 g granulated sugar

Equipment
Piping bag fitted with a ½ inch | 10 mm plain tip

Macaron shells

1. Combine the ground almonds and confectioners' sugar in a food processor and pulse to obtain a fine powder. Sift the mixture.

2. Whisk the 6 egg whites to a foam. Once frothy, add a ⅓ of the granulated sugar and whip until the sugar has dissolved. Add another ⅓ and whip for approximately 1 more minute. Finally, add the last ⅓ and whip for another minute.

3. Add a few drops of food coloring according to your recipe.

4. Delicately fold the ground almonds and confectioners' sugar into the egg whites.

5. Whip the last ½ egg white in a bowl and add to the bowl. Stir to slightly deflate the batter until it has loosened.

6. Line a baking sheet with parchment paper. Fill the piping bag with the macaron batter. Pipe small macaron mounds, 1 ¼–1 ½ inch | 3–4 mm in diameter. Lightly tap the sheet so that the macarons spread fully.

Chef's tip

It is possible that your macaron shells will crack slightly for a number of reasons, including the ingredients, the oven or how the batter was prepared.
Whatever the reason, do not be discouraged! Rest assured, cracked or not, your macarons will be just as delicious. With experience, you will succeed in making beautiful, smooth macarons.
It is strongly recommended that you allow the finished macarons to rest one night in the refrigerator.
During this time, a reaction takes place between the ingredients, further enhancing and refining the flavor and texture.

7. Preheat the oven to 300°F | 150°C | gas mark 2. Allow the macarons to sit uncovered for 20 minutes before placing them in the oven. Bake for approximately 14 minutes.

8. Remove the baking sheet from the oven.
Lift each corner of the paper slightly, one after the other and using a small glass, carefully pour a very small amount of water between the sheet and the parchment paper.
The moisture and steam produced by the water on the hot baking sheet will allow you to peel off the macarons more easily once they are cool. Allow to cool completely.

9. Peel off the shells and place them upside down on a plate, and store in the fridge overnight.

Basic Recipes

Pastry cream

Makes 5 cups | 600 g pastry cream
Preparation: 30 minutes
Cooking time: 5 minutes

1 vanilla pod
1 ⅔ cups | 400 ml whole milk
4 organic egg yolks
½ cup(minus)1 tbsp | 80 g granulated sugar
¼ cup | 30 g cornstarch (cornflour)
2 tbsp | 25 g butter

1. With a sharp knife, slice the vanilla bean in half lengthwise. Using the tip, scrape the interior to remove the seeds. Pour the milk into a saucepan, add the vanilla pod and seeds. Bring to a simmer. Remove from heat, cover and leave to infuse for 15 minutes.

2. In a bowl, whisk the egg yolks and sugar until the mixture pales slightly. Incorporate the cornstarch.
Remove the vanilla pod from the saucepan and bring the milk back to a gentle simmer. Pour ⅓ of the hot milk over the egg yolk, sugar, cornstarch mixture and whisk thoroughly. Pour the egg mixture back into the saucepan and bring to a boil while stirring constantly with the whisk, making sure to scrape down the sides of the pan with a spatula.

3. Remove the cream from heat and pour it into a bowl. Allow to cool for 10 minutes. It should be hot but not scalding. Add butter while stirring. Cover the bowl with plastic wrap until ready to use.

The Ladurée Tea Collection

OUR CREATIONS

Mélange Ladurée
The house blend. An elegant combination of Chinese black tea, citrus, flowers, gentle spices and vanilla. A delicious, delicate mouth-watering blend.
Ladurée's trademark tea.

Marie-Antoinette
A gracious combination of Chinese black tea with rose petals, citrus and honey, evoking the bucolic beauty of Versailles.
An afternoon tea.

Joséphine
A black tea from China with citrus notes – mandarin, grapefruit, orange and lemon – delicately enhanced with jasmine flowers.
A refined elegant blend.
Any time of the day.

Eugénie
A Chinese black tea with red fruits – strawberry, raspberry, cherry and redcurrants – to create a deliciously aromatic yet gentle brew.
An afternoon tea.

Othello
An Indian black tea with hints of cinnamon, cardamom, pepper and ginger. A powerful full-bodied tea.
A day tea.

Chéri
Chinese black tea with cocoa, caramel and vanilla to create a warm romantic blend redolent of Colette's novel Chéri.
A five o'clock tea.

Roi Soleil
A green tea enhanced with bergamot and hints of rhubarb and caramel.
A royal blend with panache.
Any time of the day.

Mathilde
A blend of green and black teas from China with orange blossom and magnolia to create a delicate, light tea, full of character.
A tea to accompany meals.

Mille et Une Nuits
Our tribute to the Arabian Nights. This gentle, spiced, Chinese green tea, blended with rose, orange blossom, mint and ginger will take you on a journey to the voluptuous, bewitching aromas of the East.
An afternoon tea.

Jour de fête
A bewitching blend of Indian black tea with cinnamon, pink peppercorns and cardamom, creating a smooth, spicy, festive tea.
Suitable throughout the day.

Vénus

A declaration of love.
A delicate aromatic green tea blended with cornflower and violet petals. The perfect tea for a daydream.
An afternoon tea.

Mistinguette

A blend of Chinese and Indonesian black teas with aromas of rose, blackcurrant and cornflower petal.
A tea to be drunk throughout the day.

Earl Grey Rose

A light Chinese green tea scented with bergamot and sprinkled with rose petals. An exceptional, fragrant tea with a gentle, feminine touch.
The perfect afternoon tea.

THE IRRESISTIBLES

Caramel

A delicious blend of Indian, Chinese and Ceylon black teas with hint of caramel and marigold.
The perfect tea to accompany that five o'clock pastry moment.

Amande

A charismatic almond tea and a tribute to the famous Ladurée macaron. A delicious smooth blend of Indian, Chinese and Ceylon teas combined with delicate dried almonds and almond essence.
Perfect with macarons. Perfect for any time of the day.

Rose

A refined, delectable tea, redolent of English gardens. Chinese and Ceylon teas blended with rose petals.
An afternoon tea.

Jardin Bleu Royal

A gracious blend of Chinese and Sri Lankan black teas with aromas of wild strawberry, rhubarb, cherry, cornflower petals and marigold to bring an explosion of fruit, with floral aromas.
A tea to be savored throughout the day.

Vanille

Chinese black tea flavored with vanilla from Madagascar. A tea time treat.
Throughout the day.

Violette

A tender delicate blend with a bouquet that develops deliciously in the teapot, composed of Chinese Oolong with violet petals.
For a rare moment of wonder.

Jasmin

Ladurée's own Jasmine blend. A delicious flavorsome treasure with a smooth mysterious aroma. Chinese green tea with freshly harvested jasmine flowers from the prestigious Grand Garden of Yin Hao.
An afternoon tea.

Fleur d'Oranger

A delicious blend of Chinese semi-fermented Oolong and orange blossom.
Provides a moment of grace amid a busy day.

Mûre

This blend of black Chinese tea and wild blackberries affords all the bucolic charm of a late-summer ramble through the brambles.
Delicious with chocolate dessert.

THE CLASSICS

Ceylon
A classic blend of black teas from Ceylon (Sri Lanka). Ceylon's long slender leaves create a robust tea, fairly high in theine, with woody artichoke notes.
Perfect for breakfast or early afternoon.

Breakfast Tea
A tonic combination of broken leaf black teas from Sri Lanka (Ceylon) and India. A strong, full-bodied brew which can be drunk like an English Breakfast Tea: with milk.
Perfect for breakfast.

Darjeeling
A perfect blend of black leaves from the legendary gardens of Darjeeling at the foothills of the Himalayas, with its notes of almond and ripe peaches.
A perfect breakfast or five o'clock tea.

Earl Grey
A unique blend of Chinese, Sri Lankan and Indian black teas delicately enhanced with bergamot essential oil from Calabria in Italy.
A breakfast tea.

Lapsang Souchong
This celebrated black tea from China, with its elegant long leaves, is smoked immediately after harvest. Its hallmark smoked flavor makes it a magnificent accompaniment for fish and chicken.
A lunchtime tea.

Senchayamato
A green tea from Japan with grassy, marine notes and a delicate hint of blackcurrant. *A refreshing pick-me-up.*

Yunnan
From the Chinese province of Yunnan, this tea with its beautiful long leaves has delicious notes of tobacco and malt that will delight tea lovers everywhere.
Low in theine, it can be drunk all day long.

Index

A

Avocado slices	214
Avocado toast	84

B

Bagels and salmon	274
Beet Tartare	182
Bostocks	220
Brioche	94
Bugnes	288
Buns (cinnamon-raisin)	216

C

Cake (chocolate-orange)	64
Cannelés (Bordeaux)	126
Carrots with Zaatar goat cheese - cocktail bites	120
Cat's tongues	254
Cheesecake	286
Club Sandwich (Ladurée)	54
Creminis (stuffed) – cocktail bites	122
Crêpes	194
Croque-madame	244
Cucumber and salmon rillettes - cocktail bites	118
Custard tart	98

D

Doughnuts	292

E

Eggs (mimosa)	58

F

Falafels	210
Financiers	36
Finger sandwiches (Beaufort)	50
Finger sandwiches (chicken)	53
Finger sandwiches (grilled vegetables)	52
Finger sandwiches (ham)	50
Finger sandwiches (salmon)	52
Fraisier	130
French toast	190
Fruit salad	34

G

Gingerbread	198
Granola (Ladurée)	92

L

Lobster rolls	278

M

Macarons - cocktail (carrot)	248
Macarons - cocktail (foie gras)	251
Macarons - cocktail (Parmesan)	250
Macarons - cocktail (salmon)	252
Macarons (chocolate and coffee)	136
Madeleines (Earl Grey)	32
Meringues	170
Mini-hamburgers	282

O

Omelette (Ladurée)	88

P

Palmiers	224
Potatoes and caviar – cocktail bites	123

R

Radish and red tuna - cocktail bites	124
Rose (cream puffs)	262
Rose (loaf cake)	158

S

Salmon filet	240
Salmon rillettes and tapioca chips	186
Savarins	140
Savory cakes (pastrami)	154
Savory cakes (summer garden)	152
Savory cakes (Tomato, Olive, Mozzarella)	155
Scallop carpaccio	28
Shortbread (cinnamon-hazelnut)	228
Shortbread (Viennese)	62

T

Tart (Raspberry-Passion fruit)	162
Tartlets (all chocolate)	258
Tartlets (Beaufort)	110
Tartlets (chives)	117
Tartlets (pastrami)	115
Tartlets (salmon)	116
Tartlets (taramasalata)	114
Tartlets (toasted seeds)	113
Tarts (lime and coconut)	70
Tarts (upside down apple)	166
Tuna (red) with satay sauce and sprouted leeks	24

Basic Recipes

Cream puff dough	299
Macaron shells	302
Pastry cream	301
Puff pastry dough	298
Shortcrust pastry dough	296
Sweet almond pastry dough	300

Acknowledgments

Ladurée would like to thank all its teams especially our pastry creator Claire Heitzler and savories director Jean Sevegnes, and their teams, as well as Guillaume Kern, Anthony Coquereau and Lucie Leroy for their pastry creations, Pierre Leballeur who wrote the pastry recipes, Thibaud Cucherat, Nicolas Le Padellec, Stevan Seva, Jérôme Basso and Clara Laurent for plate arrangement and visual design, Aurélie Bugaud, Sylviane Banchon and Eglantine Chaignaud, who wrote the savory recipes.

We also wish to thank the creative director Safia Thomass and the Thé brand communication and marketing chiefs, Aude Schlosser and Anne Loizeau Gitlis.

We are also grateful to Ladurée's sales directors, Vanessa Kalus and Nicolas Desgrippes, for their precious assistance.

For their role in photography design, **Christèle Ageorges** and **Marie-Pierre Morel** wish to thank:
Silverware: Ercuis. **Tableware**: Atelier Murmur, Atelier Singulier, Bernardaud, Craftslab, Elsa Le Saux, Gien, Haviland, Jars Céramistes, JL Coquet, Le Fiacre Anglais, Le Sentiment des Choses, Marie Daâge, Nakaniwa, Raynaud. **Candles**: Cire Trudon Chairs: The Conran Shop.
Table linen: Le Jacquard Français. **Other linen**: Bertozzi.
Objets d'art and Russian crafts: Peterhof Stationery.
La Petite Papeterie Française, Madeleine and Gustave.
Porcelain and antique silverware: Au Bain Marie

First published in the English language in 2017 by **THE VENDOME PRESS**

Vendome is a registered trademark of The Vendome Press, LLC

NEW YORK	LONDON
Studio 2043	63 Edith Grove
244 Fifth Avenue	London, UK
NY 10011	SW10 0LB
www.vendomepress.com	www.vendomepress.co.uk

Publishers: Beatrice Vincenzini, Mark Magowan & Francesco Venturi

Copyright © 2017 The Vendome Press and CO & Bear Productions (UK) Ltd

First published in French by
© 2017, Editions du Chêne – Hachette Livre for the original edition

Translation © Co & Bear Productions (UK) Ltd, 2017
Translation by Jonno Slysa and Ly Lan Dill
English layout : Vincent Lanceau

Editorial Manager: Valérie Tognali, assisted by Sandrine Rosenberg
Editor: Aude Le Pichon
Artistic Director: Sabine Houplain
Design and Layout: Caroline Racoupeau
Production: Marion Lance
Proofreader: Rosalind Fairclough

Distributed in North America by Abrams Books
Distributed in the rest of world by Thames & Hudson

ISBN 978-0-86565-346-7

First Edition
10 9 8 7 6 5 4 3 2 1

Library of Congress Cataloging-in-Publication Data is available upon request.

Color separation: Reproscan
Printed in China

All rights reserved. No part of the contents of this book may be reproduced in whole or in part without prior written permission from the publisher.